Counselling Athletes

Reversal theory is an innovative psychological theory exploring human motivation, emotion and personality. This is the first book in the field to examine how reversal theory can be used by practitioners in applied sport psychology in their counselling work with athletes.

Counselling Athletes explores the key elements of reversal theory, and comprehensively demonstrates how reversal theory can improve understanding in the following key areas:

- athletes' motivational characteristics
- athletes' motivational states when performing
- identifying performance problems
- athletes' experiences of stress
- intervention strategies
- eating disorders
- exercise addiction

Each chapter includes real-life case study material from elite performers in sport, as well as guides to further reading and questions for discussion.

Counselling Athletes is essential reading for practising sport psychologists and coaches, and for any student of sport psychology.

John Kerr is a professor of sport psychology at Tsukuba University in Japan.

Counselling Athletes

Applying reversal theory

John H. Kerr

London and New York

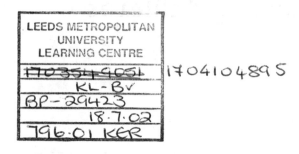
First published 2001
by Routledge, an imprint of Taylor & Francis
11 New Fetter Lane, London EC4P 4EE

Simultaneously published in the USA and Canada
by Routledge
29 West 35th Street, New York, NY 10001

Routledge is an imprint of the Taylor & Francis Group

© 2001 John H. Kerr; appendix © 2001 Oscar Randall Braman

Typeset in Times by Keystroke, Jacaranda Lodge, Wolverhampton
Printed and bound in Great Britain by TJ International Ltd, Padstow, Cornwall

British Library Cataloguing in Publication Data
A catalogue record for this book is available from the British Library

Library of Congress Cataloging in Publication Data
Kerr, J.H.
    Counselling athletes: applying reversal theory / John H. Kerr.
      p.cm.
    Includes bibliographical references and index.
    1. Sports–Psychological aspects. 2. Reversal theory (Psychology)
    3. Athletes–Counseling of. I. Title.

    GV706.4 .K465 2001
    616.89'088'796–dc21   2001018069

ISBN 0–419–26120–6 (hbk)
ISBN 0–419–26130–3 (pbk)

For
Freddy and Mitch

Contents

Illustrations

Figures

Tables

Preface

Previous books on reversal theory and sport have concentrated on theoretical issues and research results. This book examines the use of reversal theory (Apter, 1982, 1989) in psychological practice. It focuses on the ways in which reversal theory can be used to understand athlete behaviour and in the design of intervention programmes for assisting sport psychologists in counselling athletes.

As reversal theory explanations of athlete behaviour are becoming better known in contemporary sport psychology, the popularity of the theory is steadily increasing, because many of those who encounter it find that it explains what they themselves have experienced in sport. Reversal theory seems to make sense, explaining psychological experience far more satisfactorily than other current theories in psychology.

The same is true of reversal theory sport research, which has now been carried out with athletes across a very wide range of sports. Reversal theory explanations of the research results are not only providing greater insight into understanding athletes' motivation, emotion and personality, but also providing confirmation of the validity of the ideas and arguments put forward by the theory.

According to the *Oxford Advanced Learner's Dictionary*, the word *counsel* means to give professional advice to somebody with a problem. Although I believe that there are athletes who can perform to their maximum without seeking psychological advice and many who are capable of dealing with any problems which may occur along the way, I also know from personal experience that there are some athletes who can benefit from psychological counselling.

I well remember teammates and opponents from my own time playing rugby who were physically gifted and extremely talented, but who never quite fulfilled their potential because of some psychologically-based problem. First, there was Steve, a magical outhalf who had all the skills necessary for the position. He could pass with precision, kick with accuracy, he had tremendous speed and a sidestep that left opponents floundering. However, as his team's play-maker he had enormous problems in decision-making and, more often than not, he called the wrong move or took the wrong option. Second, there was Alan, a young, developing fullback who, as well as being a better than average rugby player, had good soccer skills. He was his team's designated place kicker and had a sound technique, was accurate and had the ability to kick the ball huge distances. However, Alan too had a problem. In important games when the pressure was on, his concentration and control deserted him and his kicking fell apart, letting himself and his teammates down when it really mattered. Third, there was Pete, a strong, abrasive, hard-tackling backrow forward who was headed for the top. He loved to play the game, but his attitude to fitness training and skills practice left much to be desired. He could never take training seriously, often approaching it in a half-hearted manner or skipping it entirely. This caused problems with his teammates and the coach. Eventually Pete lost his place in the team, became demotivated and stopped playing rugby. There were others, but these three examples serve to illustrate my point.

This was nearly twenty years ago, at a time when sport psychology and other sport sciences were just becoming recognised as important by coaches and sporting bodies. Athletes were sceptical about psychology, and practising sport psychologists were just not available in adequate numbers at that time. I am certain, however, that if those three rugby athletes had had an opportunity to meet with a sport psychologist, they might well have received the advice they required to overcome their performance problems and fulfilled their true potential. Now, in the year 2001, the attitude to sport psychology has changed enormously and in this book, for example, we meet many athletes who have benefited in a number of ways from sport psychology counselling.

Some authors have argued that the relationship between athlete and sport psychologist is very similar to the relationship between client and counsellor in non-sport contexts (e.g. Pepitas *et al.* 1999). In addition, Dryden and Feltham (1992) believe that there is no essential distinction between counselling and psychotherapy: 'We disagree with commentators who define counselling as a superficial, brief, symptom-removing activity which compares unfavourably with the "real" work of (long-term and "in-depth") psychotherapy' (p. 2). A similar stance is taken here. It is believed that much of the successful reversal theory work carried out in psychotherapy and client counselling can be successfully applied to the counselling of athletes. In addition, it is assumed that most athlete counselling will take the form of what Dryden and Feltham (1992) have termed 'brief counselling', which is any counselling that lasts from one session to a maximum of approximately twenty sessions.

This book relies heavily on the use of case material from athletes' actual sport experiences. The material has not been artificially manufactured to argue a particular view, or make a specific point, but concerns real occurrences. Bromley (1986, p. 3) has defined a psychological case study as 'an account of how and why a person behaved as he or she did in a given situation'. A case report is a spoken or written account of a case study and case vignettes are very brief case reports. All three comprise part of the idiographic approach to personality study (Bromley, 1986), and all three are used in this book. This case material has been organised in a consistent format, beginning with some background information about the athlete and going on to cover the content of the athlete's consultations with a sport psychologist, a reversal theory interpretation of the content, the intervention strategy implemented by the sport psychologist and, finally, a summary of the outcome of that intervention.

Recently, the British Olympic Association found it necessary to publish a position statement on athlete confidentiality (British Olympic Association, 2000). Among those who produced the statement were the chairs of the sport science and sport medicine steering groups of the British Olympic Association and other UK professional sport science and sport medicine bodies, as well as legal advisers. It was aimed at coaches, managers, administrators and medical support staff, and other sport scientists, including psychologists. It would appear that not everyone has been respecting athletes' rights and the confidentiality of information concerning them. Material like that included in psychological case studies is private and can be sensitive. Francis (1999) pointed out, 'The client has a right to have details of his or her consultancy kept confidential except where such information is required to be divulged by law' (pp. 87–88). In this text, the athletes concerned consented to having their case material published under the condition of anonymity (with the exception of one athlete who insisted his real name be published). In order to maintain athlete confidentiality, athletes' names have been changed and, in some instances, nationalities and specific details of the athlete's sport or particular top-level sports events and their dates have not been given. This was done to protect the athletes in line with ethical considerations about the rights of clients consulting a psychologist (Francis, 1999).

This is the fourth book on reversal theory and sport. *Motivation and Emotion in Sport: Reversal Theory* (Kerr, 1997) was concerned with the application of reversal theory to a wide range of topics in sport psychology, *Experiencing Sport: Reversal Theory* (Kerr, 1999) presented the latest research results and explored future avenues for research, while *Understanding Soccer Hooliganism* (Kerr, 1994) explored the motivation of aggressive and violent soccer hooligans. This book deals with the application of reversal theory to sport psychology practice. It should therefore be of interest to those working with athletes to improve their performance, those counselling athletes who may be experiencing problems, including practising sport psychologists, university staff and students teaching or studying sport psychology, as well as to athletes themselves.

Acknowledgements

I would like to thank many people without whose interest and help this book would not even have been started, let alone completed: the athletes who completed questionnaires or allowed themselves to be interviewed; Michelle Pain, Andrew Jago and Janet Young in Melbourne, and the others in the reversal theory special interest group in sport for the stimulating discussions we have had about reversal theory and counselling athletes. Michelle Blaydon and Jonathan Males deserve a special word of thanks, as do Mike Apter and George Wilson for their insightful comments on early drafts of the various book chapters. Once again, I am very grateful to Mieke Mitchell, who plays such a crucial role in all of my book publications. In addition, I would like to thank Simon Whitmore (and his predecessors Sally Wride and Liz Mann) and the rest of the publication team at Routledge for bringing this project to completion.

In addition, I would like to devote a special word of thanks to Dr Ken Smith, who passed away recently at the age of 89. Ken, Mike Apter's father, was the progenitor of reversal theory and the source of many of the ideas included in this book. He maintained a particular personal interest in the applications and developments of reversal theory in the understanding of human behaviour in sport. Ken, who had been a GP, a squadron leader in the RAF during World War II, a psychiatrist, a musician and songwriter, a radio entertainer and a lover of sport, was a truly remarkable man. He had the enviable knack of being able quickly to develop a rapport with people from all backgrounds, somehow immediately putting them at ease. Indeed, if I had been a war-weary pilot, a prisoner in trouble, a parent with a problem child, or an athlete who needed help and counselling, he'd have been the one I'd have chosen to go to for help.

As a rugby man, I felt a special bond with him and particularly value the many discussions we had at reversal theory conferences – not always, I might add, about reversal theory, but also about sport and more especially rugby. I regret not having been able to play rugby with him. If he had been the team captain when I was playing, I'd have wanted to be in his team. Equally, if I'd wanted to go out for a night of social activities after the match, I'd have wanted him along too. Ken was a multi-talented man and, for those of us fortunate enough to have met him through our interest in reversal theory, he has left a lasting impression on us all. I count it a great privilege to have known him.

Chapter 1

Getting started with reversal theory

THE BASICS

It is quite a challenge to summarise reversal theory, an innovative theory of motivation, emotion and personality, in a single chapter. Michael Apter's two books outlining the theory (Apter, 1982, 1989) contained 369 and 195 pages of explanatory text, respectively. This chapter will, however, take on this challenge in order to provide readers with a basic knowledge of reversal theory. Applications of the theory to counselling athletes will be developed in later chapters. Figure 1.1 shows the concepts from reversal theory that are most relevant to athlete counselling.

Step 1 in getting started with reversal theory is to note that reversal theory is a *general theory* of psychology which utilises a *structural-phenomenological* approach. In addition, the theory considers human behaviour to be inherently inconsistent and argues that *reversals* between paired *metamotivational* states form the basis of human personality, emotion and motivation. Step 2 involves examining the basic features of reversal theory, and the technical terms they have been assigned, in more detail.

STRUCTURAL PHENOMENOLOGY

Phenomenology is one of the major approaches in the study of psychology. It concentrates on the individual's subjective experience of life events. Structural phenomenology is the special form of phenomenology which is utilised by reversal theory. In structural phenomenology, the subjective experience of cognition and emotion, as well as one's own motivation, is thought to be influenced by certain structures and patterns. Thus, structural phenomenology provides a perspective on how human motivation is organised. Tied in with the individual focus of reversal theory is the notion that there is an inherent inconsistency in the way that people behave. In other words, an athlete who finds him or herself in the same situation on different occasions may behave in totally different ways.

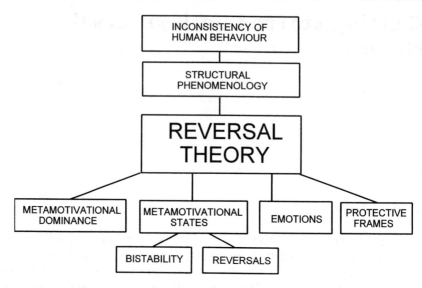

Figure 1.1 The main concepts in reversal theory which are relevant to counselling athletes (adapted from Kerr, 1994).

METAMOTIVATIONAL STATES AND REVERSALS

Metamotivational states are mental states which are concerned with how athletes experience their motives. There are eight different metamotivational states bonded together in four pairs which coexist separately within *bistable systems*. The concept of bistability has been adopted by reversal theory from cybernetics to explain the rapid changes or psychological reversals that take place backwards and forwards over time between any pair of metamotivational states. In cybernetics, a bistable system is one which tends to maintain a specified variable, despite external disturbance, within one or another of two ranges of values of the variable concerned. The four sets of partner metamotivational states are known as the *telic and paratelic*, *negativistic and conformist*, *autic and alloic*, and *mastery and sympathy* states. The first four are primarily concerned with the way an athlete experiences his or her own bodily arousal and are therefore known as the *somatic states*. The latter four states are primarily concerned with interactions with other people or, in some situations, objects (e.g. motorcycles, boats, horses, skis and other sports equipment), and have therefore been labelled the *transactional states*. In reversal theory, the relative importance of one state over the others at any particular time is known as *salience*.

An analogy might be useful in illustrating the relationship which exists between partner metamotivational states. For example, consider a viewer who is particularly interested in sport sitting down to watch television. Two sports events (e.g. track-and-field athletics and tennis) are being transmitted on different channels, say channels 1 and 2, at the same time. Although interested in both events, the person concerned can only watch athletics on channel 1 or tennis on channel 2 at any one time, but by using the remote control to switch back and forth between channels, the viewer can see the best action from both events. Here, channel 1 can be thought of as representing one metamotivational state (e.g. the telic state) and channel 2 its paired partner (e.g. the paratelic state), and the switches between channels can be thought of as the reversals which occur between metamotivational states in everyday life (see Figure 1.3, p. 5).

Characteristics of the somatic states

Telic state

With the telic state operative, an athlete's behaviour is likely to be serious, goal oriented and future related in the sense that it involves considerable planning ahead. This form of athlete behaviour is typical of many training situations where a high workrate and the completion of training goals are to the fore. Also, when in this state, athletes will generally have a preference for experiencing low levels of *felt arousal* (see 'Metamotivational variables and the sixteen primary emotions', p. 13).

Paratelic state

With the paratelic state operative, an athlete's behaviour is likely to be spontaneous, impulsive and sensation oriented, and geared to prolonging the immediate enjoyment of ongoing activities. In this state, the athlete prefers high levels of felt arousal and, where goals exist, their purpose is to add to the pleasure in a situation. Scandinavian fartlek distance running training is a good example, where fun is the main objective and distance and time are of lesser importance.

Negativistic state

Athletes in the negativistic state tend to be rebellious, stubborn and defiant, feeling the need to act against something or someone. With this state operative, an athlete might react to the aggressive barracking of rival fans and respond by directing a provocative gesture at them.

Conformist state

Athletes in the conformist state are usually agreeable and cooperative, and have a desire to comply with rules. The written and unwritten rules and conventions of many sports require compliance by the athletes concerned and, as a result, athletes will often be in the conformist state when competing.

Characteristics of the transactional states

Autic state

The focus for athletes in the autic state is themselves and what happens to them personally in any sporting or other interaction. If an athlete perceives him or herself as successful in an interaction, it is a pleasant experience; if unsuccessful, it is experienced as unpleasant. A try-saving tackle in rugby or a diving catch in the cricket outfield executed successfully would engender pleasant feelings for an athlete with the autic state operative.

Alloic state

When the alloic state is operative, the focus for an athlete is what happens to other athletes, coaching staff or even officials in any sporting interaction. Perceiving these other participants as having been successful will induce feelings of pleasure and satisfaction in that particular athlete. For example, for a player in the alloic state, a winning goal scored by a field hockey teammate in injury time at the end of a close, hard-fought game would be experienced in this way.

Mastery state

Athletes may often find themselves in the mastery state when competing against another athlete or team. In the usual competitive situation, they will feel the need to be tough and masterful in order to defeat opponents.

Sympathy state

When the sympathy state is operative, athletes will feel the need to empathise with others, perhaps teammates or supporting spectators. Here feelings of harmony and unity may be important.

Figure 1.2 shows a summary of the major characteristics of the somatic and transactional metamotivational states.

HOW REVERSALS TAKE PLACE

Reversals are thought to be involuntary and sometimes unexpected. In other words, a person cannot suddenly decide that he or she would prefer to be in, say, the telic state and consciously prompt a reversal to that state from the paratelic state. Reversal theory hypothesises that there are three ways in which reversals take place. These have been termed *contingency*, *frustration* and *satiation* (see Figure 1.3).

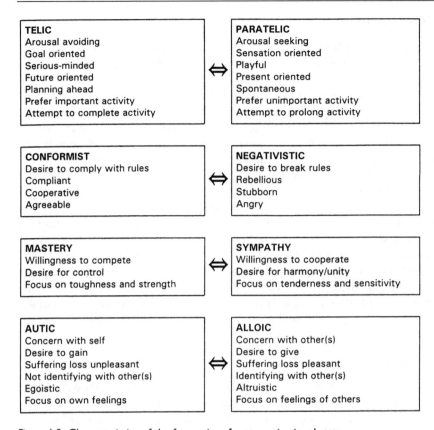

TELIC	PARATELIC
Arousal avoiding	Arousal seeking
Goal oriented	Sensation oriented
Serious-minded	Playful
Future oriented	Present oriented
Planning ahead	Spontaneous
Prefer important activity	Prefer unimportant activity
Attempt to complete activity	Attempt to prolong activity

CONFORMIST	NEGATIVISTIC
Desire to comply with rules	Desire to break rules
Compliant	Rebellious
Cooperative	Stubborn
Agreeable	Angry

MASTERY	SYMPATHY
Willingness to compete	Willingness to cooperate
Desire for control	Desire for harmony/unity
Focus on toughness and strength	Focus on tenderness and sensitivity

AUTIC	ALLOIC
Concern with self	Concern with other(s)
Desire to gain	Desire to give
Suffering loss unpleasant	Suffering loss pleasant
Not identifying with other(s)	Identifying with other(s)
Egoistic	Altruistic
Focus on own feelings	Focus on feelings of others

Figure 1.2 Characteristics of the four pairs of metamotivational states.

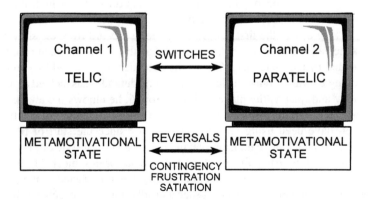

Figure 1.3 Television channel switching illustrating how reversals are induced by the three types of inducing agents.

Contingency

A club cricketer plays recreational cricket at the weekend. He is the team's best fast bowler and takes his bowling very seriously, thinking about and planning the series of balls in each over very carefully. When he is bowling, he is typically in the telic state. However, he has never shown much talent or skill with the bat and he regularly bats near the bottom of the team batting order. As a result, his attitude when batting has been to treat it as a bit of a laugh, getting to the crease and swinging his bat with reckless abandon, hoping to notch up a few lucky runs before he gets bowled out. When he is batting he is typically in the paratelic state.

During one particular match in the latter stages of a cup competition, his more talented teammates at the top and middle of the batting order fail to come to terms with a very skilful spin bowler and they are skittled out for a very low score. He finds himself going out to bat with nine wickets down. He and his partner are the last batsmen. Usually when he bats he is in the paratelic state, but now, owing to the sudden collapse of his team's normally dependable batting and the fact that he has to bat slowly and cautiously to try to achieve a good score and get his team out of trouble, he undergoes a reversal and finds himself in the telic state. In this example, the batting collapse is an environmental event which has induced a reversal from the paratelic to the telic state (e.g. Svebak *et al.*, 1982).

Frustration

A rugby league match involves two teams from a premier division, but with players of very different abilities and playing styles. One team has extremely skilful players who are intent on playing the game to the best of their ability and using team strategy and tactics which involve a flowing, entertaining game. The other team's players are not as skilful and have developed a style of play which is dependent on 'mixing it' with the opposing players and trying to upset their playing style. This often means using physically violent, unlawful tactics which they have employed with some success in previous matches.

Towards the end of the first half of the game, a forward from the skilful team receives the ball and runs at speed, trying to break through the opposition defence. He is tackled by two defenders. One of the defenders has tackled low and taken the attacking forward around the legs. The second defender has tackled around the upper body and, just as the players hit the ground, he elbows the attacker hard in the face. The foul play was unseen by referee and touch judges. In addition, the opposition have been using very dubious tactics since the start of the game, preventing the attacking team from playing their usual open style of play. This is the third or fourth time that the attacking forward has been subjected to foul play. Following the instructions of the team coach, he has not reacted to the previous incidents, remaining in the conformist state and adhering to the coach's instructions and the rules of the game. With the latest incident, however, a reversal from the conformist to the negativistic state takes place, prompted by the repeated acts of foul play. The attacking forward angrily retaliates and a punch-up between the two players develops. This time, however, the touch judge has observed the retaliation and, after consulting with the referee, the attacking forward (feeling even more aggrieved and negativistic) is sent off the pitch to the 'sinbin'. This example illustrates the second type of reversal induction, where a reversal has occurred owing to conditions of *frustration*, where an athlete has been unable to obtain satisfaction in an operative state or state combination (see, for example, Barr *et al.*, 1990).

Satiation

A professional volleyball player is a member of a team based in Japan. Prior to the start of the playing season, she participated in pre-season training and attended a special summer training camp. Once the season began, she became a permanent member of the team and played in all the team's matches. She has a very serious and dedicated approach to volleyball and when she is training and playing she usually has the telic state operative. At the end of a long season, she joined her national team at a four-day international tournament. During her last game, at a stage when the two opposing teams were evenly matched, she suddenly reversed from the telic to the paratelic state. She found herself in a rather playful mood, making unplanned, spontaneous plays. Even so, her team managed to win and returned to the dressing room. After showering and changing, the player, still with the paratelic state operative, left the volleyball facility and went out on the town for an all-night binge of drinking and partying with some of her teammates. This example illustrates the third type of reversal-inducing agent, *satiation*, which is increasingly likely to induce a reversal if an athlete has been in one metamotivational state for some time (e.g. Lafreniere *et al.*, 1988).

Although reversals are thought to be involuntary, some research evidence does suggest that people may be able to place themselves in particular situations and other contexts, or create environmental conditions which are likely to induce reversals to particular metamotivational states (e.g. Kerr and Tacon, 1999). Some examples of research which examined reversals in sport are: Cox and Kerr (1989, 1990), research on competitive squash; Kerr and Vlaswinkel (1993), a study on long-distance running; and Males and Kerr (1996), research on slalom canoeing. In addition, details of these studies and all the latest reversal theory sport research can be found in Kerr (1997, 1999).

METAMOTIVATIONAL DOMINANCE

To return to the television analogy used earlier, if the action is especially thrilling, a viewer may spend more time watching one channel than the other. In a similar way, though psychological reversals between metamotivational states are thought to take place frequently, each athlete will vary in the amount of time spent in either one of two partner states. Athletes, therefore, who have a tendency or innate bias to spend more time in one metamotivational state over its partner are said to be, for example, *telic dominant* or *mastery dominant*. Even though athletes may exhibit particular state dominances, they will reverse and spend time in their non-dominant states.

Research examining metamotivational dominance in sport has shown, for example, that telic dominance is associated with participation in and preference for endurance sports, such as long-distance running and hiking (Svebak and Kerr, 1989), and paratelic dominance with explosive sports such as baseball and cricket (Svebak and Kerr, 1989), along with risk sports such as parachuting, motorcycle racing and snow-boarding (Cogan and Brown, 1998; Kerr, 1991; and see Chapter 3).

PROTECTIVE FRAMES AND PARAPATHIC EMOTIONS

In special circumstances, where a paratelic *protective frame* exists, emotions that are usually experienced as unpleasant can be experienced as pleasant. In this form they are known as *parapathic emotions*. A protective frame is a kind of psychological bubble, or more specifically a phenomenological frame, which provides a sense of safety in dangerous situations or circumstances. According to reversal theory, it is by means of paratelic protective frames that recreational or competitive athletes involved in risk sports, such as skydiving, are able to enjoy activities which others perceive as highly dangerous. The skydiver, for example, can experience the unpleasant telic anxiety typically associated with skydiving in a pleasant form, through paratelic protective frames and parapathic emotions. Of course, if for any reason the frame should break (for example, as a result of a sudden equipment failure), the pleasant parapathic emotion (anxiety) will once again be experienced in its unpleasant form. Experiencing protective frames is synonymous with being in the paratelic state. Kerr (1997) has explored the reversal theory concept of protective frames and participation in dangerous sports, and Apter (1992) has explored the concept across the whole gamut of sport, recreational and other activities.

METAMOTIVATIONAL STATE COMBINATIONS

Step 3 in getting started with reversal theory is to examine a more complex development, that of *metamotivational state combinations* and the emotions which occur as a result.

Two-way somatic state combinations

Perhaps the best way of illustrating the concept of metamotivational state combinations is to return to the television analogy. The original setup can be extended to include two more channels. There are now four channels available to the viewer: channels 1, 2, 3 and 4. With the split-screen function that is available on some contemporary televisions, a viewer can watch two channels at the same time. However, suppose the split-screen function works in such a way that either channel 1 or 2 can be viewed on one panel and either 3 or 4 can be viewed on the other. This would mean that there are four possible split-screen combinations between which a viewer could channel-switch: channels 1 and 3, channels 1 and 4, channels 2 and 3, channels 2 and 4. Here, as well as channel 1 representing the telic state and channel 2 representing the paratelic state, channels 3 and 4 can be thought of as representing the negativistic and conformist metamotivational states, respectively (see Figure 1.4). Like the switches between channels, reversals between telic and paratelic states and between negativistic and conformist states are possible, and the different split-screen combinations represent possible metamotivational combinations of the four somatic states (telic–negativistic, telic–conformist, paratelic–negativistic, paratelic–conformist).

Some examples from sport may help to illustrate how these two-way somatic state combinations work. The paratelic–conformist state combination is likely to be operative when a person is playing a leisurely game of pool or snooker with a friend. The game finishes and they decide to play another one. However, the friend suggests that in the next game they should have a sizeable wager on the outcome. This changes the players' perception of the seriousness of the play and might well induce a reversal from the paratelic to the telic state. Thus, if a reversal does occur, the person's state combination changes from paratelic–conformity to telic–conformity (conformity because the player has to adhere to the rules and

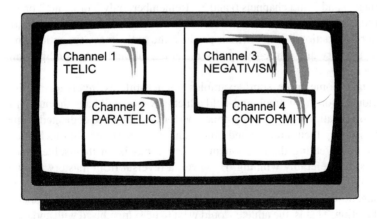

Figure 1.4 The television split screen analogy representing two-way somatic state combinations.

conventions of the game). For professional pool or snooker players involved in top-level competitions, the telic–conformist state combination would be likely to be operative because of the seriousness of the competition and the large amounts of prize money to be won by successful play.

Angry athletes who verbally abuse, push or, very occasionally, strike umpires or referees are likely to be in the telic–negativistic state combination. This usually occurs when the umpire or referee has made what the athlete considers to be an unfair decision against the athlete or the team. The abusive behaviour is a response to perceived injustice.

When athletes' behaviour involves doing something 'just for the hell of it', then it is probable that they are in a paratelic–negativistic state combination. A good example of this is the ethos of the style of play of the Barbarians rugby team (a specially selected team mostly comprised of players from England, Ireland, Scotland and Wales which plays a one-off match against visiting touring teams from other countries), which is representative of paratelic–negativism. The Barbarians' tradition is that they play in an unconventional, entertaining way, throwing caution aside and trying personal skills and team moves and tactics which they would rarely try in their regular telic–conformist-oriented matches. In this way, players can, to some extent at least, enjoy defying the usual expectations and break with the established way of doing things.

Two-way transactional state combinations

What is true for the somatic states is also true for the transactional states. Imagine a second set of four channels, again arranged in two pairs (5–6 and 7–8). Channels 5 and 6 represent the autic and alloic states and channels 7 and 8 the mastery and sympathy states, respectively. In the same way as for the four previous channels, four more channel combinations are possible: channels 5 and 7, channels 5 and 8, channels 6 and 7 and channels 6 and 8. (Remember, only 5 or 6 and 7 or 8 can be viewed at any one time). These channel combinations represent combinations of partner transactional states which produce the autic–mastery, autic–sympathy, alloic–mastery and alloic–sympathy metamotivational state combinations (see Figure 1.5).

To take some more sport examples, many athletes involved in elite-level individual sports (e.g. track-and-field athletic events) will have the autic–mastery state combination operative when they perform. They have dedicated themselves to maximising their strength and fitness and have mastered their technique, with a view to defeating their opponents. Their focus is on themselves and being successful, preferably winning. However, a reversal from mastery to sympathy state might occur if the athlete had been unluckily disqualified (e.g. for false-starting, no-throwing or no-jumping). This would result in an autic–sympathy state combination. That is, the athlete would want to be sympathised with and reassured.

Conversely, a male coach guiding his athlete or team through a tournament will most likely be in the alloic–mastery state as he instructs, guides and urges his

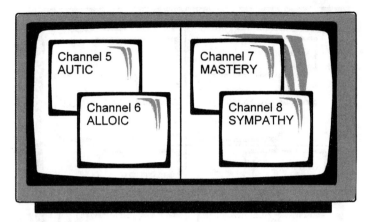

Figure 1.5 The television split screen analogy representing two-way transactional state combinations.

athlete or team towards victory. The alloic–sympathy state combination might be operative in an athlete who, after competing well, stops at the edge of the playing arena to sign autographs for admiring teenage fans.

Four-way metamotivational combinations

Imagine that the two sets of four channels in the television analogy have been added together and it is now possible for the viewer to watch four channels (one from each pair) at any one time through a four-way split screen. As shown in Figure 1.6, there are four television channels possible in any combination. This means that, for example, channels 1, 3, 5 and 8 could be viewed together, as could channels 2, 3, 6 and 8. These television channel combinations represent the metamotivational state combinations of telic–negativistic–autic–mastery and paratelic–negativistic–alloic–sympathy, respectively. Of course, these are examples; several other four-way metamotivational combinations are possible.

Reversals between partner states will occur, and so the component states within any state combination will change relatively frequently. An analogy is real-life cable television which has one channel consisting of an overview of all the other channels, often showing twelve or more channels in miniature on one regular-sized screen. As the viewer watches, the mini-channels change periodically in an apparently random organisation to show brief glimpses of the many cable channels on offer.

This arrangement of metamotivational state combinations is possible through the introduction of the concept of *multistable systems*, which, like the bistable system, also originates from cybernetics. In reversal theory, a multistable system is really a more complex version of the bistable arrangement that exists between any two partner states. The two sets of somatic states and the two sets of

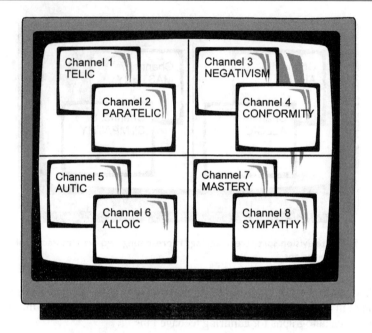

Figure 1.6 The television split screen analogy representing four-way somatic and transactional state combinations.

transactional states interact together within a multistable system. Thus, reversal theory is a multistable theory of motivation.

Four-way state combinations in sport

The Eco Challenge is a long-distance endurance team race over extremely difficult terrain which involves activities such as hiking, running, swimming, mountain biking, canoeing, rock climbing, abseiling and horse riding. The Eco Challenge is designed to be exactly that: a challenge which pushes the competing teams of three men and one woman to their absolute maximum and beyond. Team members voluntarily suffer excruciating pain from blisters, pulled muscles, cramp, injuries from falls, intense heat and cold, dehydration, lack of sleep and other, more serious medical conditions. Teams have to plan their own routes over each stage and all the teams in the race are carefully checked at regular rest and food stops. When a team or individual athlete's long-term health or, in some instances, life is threatened, organisers and medical support staff can prevent them from continuing. Back-up helicopters often have to search for competitors in trouble and airlift them back to base hospitals. All four team members have to finish the race; if one is forced to drop out, then the others have to stop as well.

The Eco Challenge provides a useful example of how metamotivational state combinations and reversals might work in the sport context. In an event like this, lasting several days, where athletes repeatedly encounter new and difficult, challenging situations, it is likely that an athlete will experience numerous different metamotivational states and state combinations. For example, when a team are planning their route for the first stage of the race, team members are likely to be in the telic and conformist states. They are also likely to have the alloic and mastery states operative as team cohesion and the desire for their colleagues to be successful is strong. At a later stage, when faced with a long and tricky abseil down a wet and slippery rock face, the athletes may find themselves firmly in a telic–conformist–autic–mastery state combination as they concentrate hard and use all their skill to personally master the task at hand.

At another stage in the race, a tired team member suffering from severe foot problems may reverse from the operative telic and mastery states to the paratelic and sympathy states, as he jokes with medical staff while they treat his cuts and blisters at a rest stop. His overall operative state combination in this situation is likely to be paratelic–conformist–autic–sympathy, with the autic–sympathy combination being most prominent. Once treatment is complete, and as the time to restart the race approaches, the athlete might reverse from paratelic to telic and from sympathy to mastery states in anticipation of what lies ahead.

In a competitive race such as this, the experience of some states may be less common than others. There would, for example, seem to be few occasions for these athletes to have the negativistic state operative. It must also be kept in mind that in a race of this kind, although certain metamotivational combinations may be operative for fairly long periods, reversals are always likely to occur as a result of sudden unexpected environmental events, frustration or satiation. For example, a fall off a mountain bike, resulting in severe scrapes and bruises, a slip from a rope while crossing a river, resulting in a complete soaking in freezing-cold water, or a canoe capsize in a choppy sea are all unexpected environmental events which might induce reversals. Also, at any one time in a metamotivational state combination, one or two states may predominate over the others. In most of the Eco Challenge race situations, the mastery state may well have been salient for many of the competitors.

METAMOTIVATIONAL VARIABLES AND THE SIXTEEN PRIMARY EMOTIONS

The preference for different levels of felt arousal in the telic and paratelic states has already been mentioned in the subsection 'Characteristics of the somatic states' (p. 3). Felt arousal is one of reversal theory's *metamotivational variables* which are associated with the different sets of partner metamotivational states. Felt arousal is the degree to which an athlete feels him or herself to be worked up. Other metamotivational variables include *felt transactional outcome* (transactional states; the degree to which a person feels him or herself to have gained or lost in an interaction); *felt significance* (telic and paratelic states; how much a person perceives a goal he or she is pursuing as significant and serving purposes beyond itself); *felt negativism* (negativistic and conformist states; how much a person feels him or herself to be acting against an external rule or requirement); and *felt toughness* (mastery–sympathy states; how much a person feels him or herself to be tough, strong or in control).

How different levels of these metamotivational variables are experienced has important implications for an athlete's experience of emotions. In this regard, felt arousal and felt transactional outcome are the two most important metamotivational variables. Felt arousal is a metamotivational variable concerned with the somatic states, and its importance in sport has been repeatedly demonstrated by reversal theory sport research (e.g. Cox and Kerr, 1989, 1990; Kerr and Cox, 1988, 1990; Kerr and Vlaswinkel, 1993; Males and Kerr, 1996).

The experience of felt arousal is dependent on whether the conformist or negativistic state is allied with the telic or paratelic state in a two-way combination. An athlete with the telic–conformist state combination operative generally prefers low levels of felt arousal. With the paratelic–conformist state combination operative, high levels of felt arousal are generally preferred. As shown in Figure 1.7, the experience of preferred levels of felt arousal is, in both cases, associated with positive hedonic tone and is experienced as pleasant *relaxation* and *excitement*, respectively. Non-preferred high levels of felt arousal in the telic state and low levels of felt arousal in the paratelic state result in negative hedonic tone and are experienced as unpleasant *anxiety* and *boredom*, respectively. Thus, there are four possible somatic emotions which may result from the experience of felt arousal conditions in the telic– or paratelic–conformist state combination.

Four additional somatic emotions are experienced when athletes are in the telic– and paratelic–negativistic state combination. In Figure 1.7, *placidity* and *provocativeness* are the two pleasant and *sullenness* and *anger* the two unpleasant emotions resulting from the various state combinations. In each case, they are also related to the experience of preferred and non-preferred levels of felt arousal, and a reversal between partner states would change the experience of arousal. For example, an athlete might be experiencing unpleasant boredom (paratelic low arousal), but a reversal to the telic state (within a two-way combination with the conformist state) would result in the low arousal then being experienced as pleasant relaxation. Equally, for the two high-arousal emotions, unpleasant telic anxiety would be experienced pleasantly as paratelic excitement if a telic to paratelic reversal took place.

Felt transactional outcome is a metamotivational variable concerned with the transactional states. As shown in Figure 1.8, a similar series of state combinations between the autic–alloic and mastery–sympathy pairs of states and the experience of felt transactional outcome in terms of net gain or loss result in the experience of eight transactional emotions. These are *pride, modesty, humiliation, shame, gratitude, virtue, guilt* and *resentment*.

The experience of metamotivational variables in both somatic and transactional state combinations contributes to hedonic tone or experienced pleasure. Provided

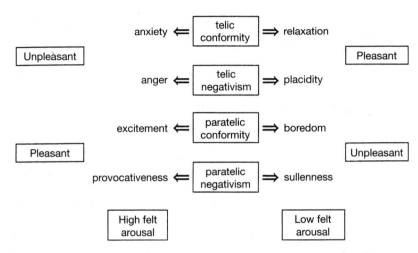

Figure 1.7 The eight somatic emotions generated by possible combinations of the telic–paratelic and negativism–conformity pairs of states (from Kerr, 1994).

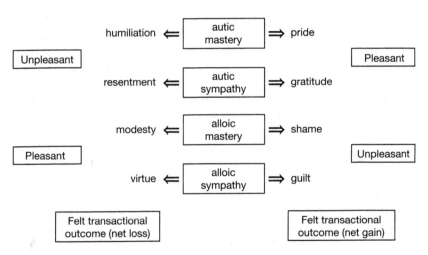

Figure 1.8 The eight transactional emotions generated by possible combinations of the autic–alloic and mastery–sympathy pairs of states (from Kerr, 1994).

reversals are not ongoing, athletes at any one time will experience one somatic and one transactional emotion, but the strength of the two emotions may vary (for example, a judo player who progresses to the quarterfinals of a tournament after injuring his or her opponent in a throw might experience mild excitement and strong guilt). Overall hedonic tone is, therefore, a composite of the two and reflects the strengths of the contributing emotions. Stress may result from mismatches in preferred and felt levels of the metamotivational variables and is reflected in low levels of hedonic tone and the experience of unpleasant emotions (see Figures 1.7. and 1.8). The reversal theory approach to stress is explained in the following, final section of the chapter.

EXPERIENCING STRESS IN SPORT

Step 4 in getting started with reversal theory focuses on how athletes experience stress and how they can attempt to cope with it. As mentioned in the previous section, any mismatch or discrepancy between felt and preferred levels of metamotivational variables, like felt arousal and felt transactional outcome, will lead to stress. For example, an archer at competition may typically perform in a specific metamotivational state combination at a preferred level of arousal. If, however, at one particular archery meet, a marked arousal discrepancy occurs between the archer's actual and preferred levels of arousal, the archer is likely to experience stress. In reversal theory there are two forms or types of stress (Svebak and Apter, 1997). The stress experienced by the archer, caused by a mismatch in preferred and felt arousal levels, is known as *tension stress*, and the effort expended by the archer in trying to reduce tension stress is known as *effort stress*. Effort stress is an attempt at coping with discrepancies in levels of metamotivational variables. For example, tension stress and effort stress can be experienced in both telic and paratelic states. In the telic state, tension stress is experienced as unpleasant threat, or anxiety, and in the paratelic state it is experienced as unpleasant lack of threat, or boredom. Effort stress in the telic state takes the form of effortful coping, but in the paratelic state it takes the form of responding to challenge(s).

In the case of the archer, let us suppose that the telic state is operative within his or her usual competitive state combination, with accompanying low levels of felt and preferred arousal. The archer will experience telic tension stress if, for example, felt arousal increases as a result of adverse weather conditions during competition. Increased felt arousal interferes with the archer's pursuance of his or her desired goals and results in unpleasant feelings of anxiety. These unpleasant feelings may lead to effort stress as the archer initiates compensatory coping behaviour aimed at reducing tension and minimising interference in his or her attempts at goal achievement.

Conversely, consider the triple jumper whose preferred performance state combination includes the paratelic state with accompanying high felt and preferred arousal. If, for example, at a certain athletics meet, injury forces the withdrawal of the jumper's main rival, the triple jumper's levels of felt arousal may become lower, and the resultant mismatch in arousal levels will be experienced as unpleasant paratelic tension stress. Instead of the competition being challenging and exciting, it is now experienced by the triple jumper as boring. In order to offset the paratelic tension stress, the triple jumper needs to initiate some form of present-oriented coping activity (experienced as paratelic effort stress) in an attempt to increase his or her level of felt arousal. This might take the form of setting up other challenges, such as trying to beat his or her personal best distance, or perhaps making an attempt at a new record.

For an athlete experiencing telic or paratelic tension stress, there are a number of options for manipulating or managing arousal levels, for example through cognitive intervention. Many sport psychology texts (e.g. Morris and Summers, 1995; Murphy, 1995) suggest that an athlete, like the archer above, experiencing anxiety (telic tension stress) could adopt an arousal reduction strategy such as a self-relaxation technique (Jacobson, 1974) to reduce his or her level of felt arousal. However, this type of intervention would be completely counter-productive for an athlete, like the triple jumper, experiencing paratelic tension stress. It is not a lowering of felt arousal which is required in this case, but the opposite, some form of arousal-enhancing strategy aimed at increasing felt arousal levels.

Another effective option for the athlete experiencing telic or paratelic tension stress is not to attempt to modulate felt arousal levels, but to induce a reversal to the partner metamotivational state. This would allow a reinterpretation of arousal levels and a subsequent reduction in tension stress, as any mismatch in felt and preferred arousal levels is corrected. Figure 1.9 summarises the two options for cognitive intervention available to the athlete experiencing either telic or paratelic tension stress.

In the examples used above, felt arousal was the metamotivational variable and telic and paratelic forms of tension stress were discussed. Equally, the other metamotivational variables and other forms of tension stress could have been used. It should be possible to modulate levels of felt transactional outcome and even felt

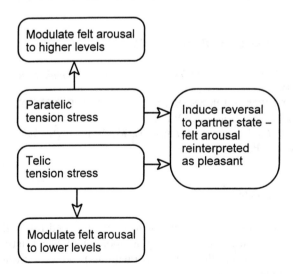

Figure 1.9 The four available options for alleviating tension stress.

negativism and felt toughness, or induce reversals between the partner states. Prior to the implementation of any of the possible intervention strategies described above, it is essential that the coach and the athlete are able to determine when the performer is experiencing different forms of tension stress.

Incidentally, reversal theory predicts that athletes' stress response may be influenced by their metamotivational dominance. Research by Summers and Stewart (1993), following on from the work of Martin *et al.* (1987), which examined dominance and the stress response in a general non-sport sample, has confirmed this prediction, showing that, while telic-dominant athletes prefer low levels of stress, paratelic–dominant athletes actually enjoy moderate levels of stress. In Chapter 6, examples of mismatches in metamotivational variables and different forms of tension stress will be discussed in detail.

CLOSING COMMENTS

If the challenge of summarising reversal theory in a single chapter has been successful, the reader should now have a good grasp of its basic concepts and be ready to proceed to subsequent chapters with confidence. For those who already had some knowledge of the theory, it is hoped that this chapter might have acted as a kind of refresher course. To put it another way, the manual has been read; now it is time to progress further with some 'hands-on' experience of how reversal theory is used in practice for counselling athletes. Like most manuals or reference texts, Chapter 1 is a source to be consulted when the need arises as progress is made through the rest of the book. Chapter 2 will deal with recognising metamotivational states and state combinations through the use of real-life examples.

SUGGESTED FURTHER READING

Apter, M. J. (2001) *Motivational Styles in Everyday Life: A Guide to Reversal Theory*, Washington, DC: American Psychological Association.
Frey, K. P. (1999) 'Reversal theory: basic concepts', in J. H. Kerr (ed.) *Experiencing Sport: Reversal Theory*, Chichester: Wiley.
Apter, M. J. (1982) *The Experience of Motivation: The Theory of Psychological Reversals*, London: Academic Press, chapters 1–5.

FOR DISCUSSION

1   Think of instances when you might have experienced reversals, either in everyday life or while participating in sport or physical activity. Try to remember the details of the particular situation(s) and what it was that might have induced the reversal.

2   Consider which metamotivational states might have been operative before any reversals you may have experienced and which states were operative after the reversal(s).

3   How did any emotions you might have been experiencing change as a result of the reversal(s)? What effect did the reversal(s) have on your overall level of hedonic tone?

Chapter 2

Recognising athletes' motivational states

INTRODUCTION

According to reversal theory, observation of a person's behaviour cannot necessarily provide an accurate insight into the thinking and motivation behind the behaviour. Japanese motorcycle rider Tomomi Manako's behaviour at the 1996 Catalonian Grand Prix provides a good illustration of why reaching conclusions about motivation based on observation of behaviour should be avoided. In celebrating his first win, Manako stunned and angered local fans by repeatedly grasping one arm at the elbow with his other hand and raising an outstretched finger. Manako later tried to explain that he had not realised his gesture was a traditional Latin insult, but that he had been trying to indicate that he was number one. The crowd observed Manako's mistaken behaviour and misunderstood what his motive had been.

What people say, provided there is a degree of certainty that they are speaking the truth, can be used as a much more accurate way of determining their motivation. This means that what athletes might reveal in personal conversations or in reliable television or newspaper interviews can be a useful source of information for those involved in sport psychology. For example, in the post-match meeting with the press that top tennis players are obliged to attend, they are often asked about details of their performances, or to describe their feelings at particular moments in matches.

In fact, in the series of examples dealing with sport scenarios presented in this chapter, numerous quotations from athletes are included. These examples are designed to aid in the recognition of operative metamotivational states and state combinations as they apply in the sport context. In Section A, each of the first group of quotations is accompanied by a reversal theory interpretation. In Section B, extracts from an interview conducted with Ross, a 27-year-old Canadian karate black belt, are used to show how interviews with athletes can be used, in a more reliable way than short quotations, to recognise metamotivational states and dominance.

SECTION A

Read each quotation, examining what was said in the light of the reversal theory interpretation placed below each example.

Davis Cup tennis

Prior to the 1999 centenary Davis Cup tennis tournament match with Britain, Jim Courier, former number one and experienced US professional, said:

> We have a job to do, we come here, we prepare and try to do the job and that's it.
>
> ('Davis Cup', 1999)

Reversal theory interpretation

Courier's comments indicate a serious, planned, goal-oriented approach to the match with Britain and have an obvious telic orientation.

French rugby

French rugby union flyhalf Thomas Castaignède was quoted as saying:

> When I play for France I try to treat it as a bit of a joke, because I'm best when I'm playing for pleasure.
>
> (Welland, 1996)

Reversal theory interpretation

In contrast to Courier's comments above, Castaignède's words have a non-serious, playful, fun approach indicative of the paratelic state.

Marathon winner

In February 1998, 27-year-old Gert Thys, a South African marathon runner, won the Tokyo International Marathon. He covered the course between Tokyo's National Stadium and Omori Beach, near Haneda Airport, and back in 2:06:33. He easily broke the course record and missed the world record of 2:06:05, held by Brazilian Ronaldo Da Costa, by only 28 seconds. After the race he said:

> It's a personal best, so I'm delighted at the time. I knew I'd got the race in the bag when I got past the Japanese runners.
>
> ('Thys runs', 1998)

Reversal theory interpretation

This quotation illustrates the pleasure and satisfaction associated with goal achievement in the telic state and Thys's positive hedonic tone as a result of improving his personal best time for the marathon. Thys may also have had the mastery state operative, indicated by his confidence in victory once he had beaten the Japanese runners.

Cricket World Cup

Australia were drawn against India in the first 'Super Six' match of the 1999 Cricket World Cup. The match appeared to be a contest between India's batsmen Sachin Tendulkar, Rahul Dravid and Saurav Ganguly, and Australia's bowling attack led by Glenn McGrath and Shane Warne. Although there was a lot at stake in the match and neither side could afford to lose, fast bowler McGrath said:

> I am really looking forward to the challenge of bowling to Sachin. It would be good to pick him up. . . . I enjoy bowling to the best batsmen in the world.
> ('Battle lines', 1999)

Reversal theory interpretation

McGrath's emphasis on the challenge of the forthcoming match suggests the paratelic state and the emphasis on enjoyment suggests positive hedonic tone.

Champion sprinter

Following a long and successful track season in 1999, world champion sprinter Maurice Greene easily won the 100 metres at the 1999 Super Track Meet in Tokyo. After the race he talked to the press:

> From today, my schedule is REST! . . . I'll take one month to enjoy the time off and look back on a wonderful season I had, and get ready and prepared for a better year than I had this year. I'll be going into next season just like I did this year . . . very confident and very strong. . . .
> But my main priority next year is to win the gold medal. . . . If the [world] record comes, great but that's not the focus. Winning gold [in the Olympics] is. It's something I haven't done, and it's something I want very bad.
> (Ohmura, 1999)

Reversal theory interpretation

After a long, telic-oriented, record-chasing season, Greene is determined to take a timeout for rest, shifting or reversing into a period when the paratelic state is likely to be operative a good deal of the time, before coming back to goal- and future-oriented chasing of Olympic gold, representative of telic functioning. Note also that the phrase 'very confident and very strong', denoting the mastery state, featured in his comments.

Positional change

In 1998 Tim Rodber switched playing positions, after winning thirty-two international rugby union caps as a backrow player:

> I had no idea I'd enjoy playing second row so much. There's a bit of stigma about the position. The second row is not the most glamorous of positions, and I never fancied it. It was too much donkey work for my liking. . . .
>
> I was a bit negative about it at first. It felt – wrongly – a little like a demotion. I felt as if I was being told I wasn't good enough in the back row, so maybe I should try somewhere else. It's fair to say there was a reluctance on my part. I wanted to stay in my own comfort zone, and even at the start of this season I was convinced I should be the England No. 8. . . .
>
> Now I see myself as a lock forward. . . . My rugby's been given a new direction and I'm excited.
>
> (Stafford, 1999)

Reversal theory interpretation

Rodber's description of his renewed interest in playing as a result of a positional change is typical of paratelic–conformist high felt arousal in the form of excitement and resultant positive hedonic tone. When the change was first made, though, he experienced an autic–sympathy-oriented reaction and probably some resentment as a result of perceived transactional loss.

Ski race accident

Russian downhill skier Tatiana Lebedeva was badly injured in a horrific collision with a race official at the 1996 World Alpine Skiing championships in Spain. She stated in a hospital interview:

> I'm in a positive frame of mind, but it is very difficult. I have all these feelings in my mind, pain and fear and so on. . . . I'll have to conquer that, but I don't know how. I just really wish it could have happened in some other way because as skiers you stand at the starting line and you are sure, you have to be sure, that the course is safe and you can go the full 100 percent. It will be difficult to turn back to confront this fear.
>
> ('Injured skier', 1996)

Reversal theory interpretation

Lebedeva's fear is recognisable as a high-arousal experience with the telic–conformist state combination operative, produced by pain and/or the threat of future injury. More than this, however, her perception that ski race courses are safe and the paratelic protective or safety frame that allowed her to ski flat out at 100 per cent has probably been shattered. She says herself that she does not know how to conquer her fear, and there is a strong likelihood that, if she cannot conquer it and re-establish the safety frame, she will never race successfully again.

Illegal tactics?

Mike Tyson met Evander Holyfield in a World Boxing Association heavyweight title fight in June 1997. Tyson was disqualified for biting both of Holyfield's ears. Apparently, Tyson believed Holyfield was using his head illegally and referee Mills Lane hadn't warned Holyfield. Six months later, in an interview Tyson said:

> As long as I live I will regret what happened that night. . . . But I cannot change anything, I can only start again and hope that I get another chance. I tasted blood that night when I bit the ear of Evander Holyfield. Yes, I went over the edge. I felt I had been pushed back into the streets. . . .
>
> Why did I do it? . . . You have to understand I grew up in the streets. I didn't have any protection, a lot of my friends died or went to prison. Our role models were drug dealers and pimps. . . . That's not an excuse, but I have to explain there were no rules. You just had to survive, hurt someone who wanted to hurt you.
>
> ('Tyson admits', 1998)

Reversal theory interpretation

The negativistic state is likely to have been salient here. Holyfield's tactics and Tyson's perception that the referee was allowing illegal use of the head provoked a response of the type recognised by reversal theorists as reactive negativism. Even in professional boxing, such a savage response suggests that Tyson was extremely angry, an emotion associated with very high arousal in a telic–negativistic state combination. The autic and mastery states may also have played a role.

Australian Rules apology

Australian Rules footballers Peter Everit, St Kilda ruckman, and opposing defender Scott Chisholm had an altercation during a match. In the incident, Everit verbally abused Chisholm, an Aboriginal player. Following a marathon four-hour hearing and a mediation session, the pair attended a media conference at AFL headquarters to announce the resolution that Everit had decided to suspend himself for four weeks. Everit admitted that he had made several racially motivated remarks to Chisholm, saying:

> I'd just like to apologize to Scott, his family and also the aboriginal and broader community for references I made during the game.
>
> ('Player suspends himself', 1999)

Reversal theory interpretation

When Everit made his apology, it seems most likely that the metamotivational state combination of alloic–sympathy was operative and that the player was feeling guilty about his verbal abuse. If, however, Everit was feeling ashamed, a state combination of alloic–mastery would have been operative.

Creative player

An interview with Brad Fittler, top Australian rugby league player, appeared in *Inside Sport* magazine. When asked about his sometimes poor defensive positioning and low work rate, and if he could play like Brad Clyde, an 'automaton-type' player, he answered:

> Nah. Don't want to do it. Not my go. . . . I just reckon the game sort of gets a bit boring if you just want to keep on hitting it up. So I'd rather try to create stuff. It makes you feel like you are having an impact.
>
> (Williams, 1995)

Reversal theory interpretation

The essence of Fittler's remarks is about creativity in the paratelic state. He finds the routine defensive play boring (paratelic–conformist, low felt arousal) and would rather use his skills to, for example, make a break or set up a play. If successful, this would probably increase his level of felt arousal, allowing him to experience a thrill and make him feel that he had an important role to play in the game.

'Erg' Championships

Joe Glickman, writing in *The Tribune*, describes his participation in the 1998 Concept II Ergometer, or 'Erg' Championships, held at the New York Athletic Club Boathouse. The Concept II is a type of flywheel rowing machine used by rowers and fitness fanatics all over the world. Using the machine involves minimal technique, no locomotion, but a great deal of pain. His division was 'heavyweight masters', with about forty competitors aged 30 to 39. Here is his account of the race:

After an anxious wait, the gun went off, and I pulled. With the crowd and adrenaline, the first two minutes felt easy, despite the fact that I was going faster than I ever had. Two minutes later, my lower back hurt, my ham-strings burned, my lungs really, really hurt, and I was slowing down. With 800 meters to go, lactic acid surged through my self-deluded veins. I heard the crowd urging me on. 'You're ahead,' came the cry, 'Pull!' After what seemed like an eternity, I was done. My time for 2,000 meters was 6 minutes 20.3 seconds, I slumped over, a wheezing shell. But when I looked up, I noticed that every-one else was still rowing. I had won! What a great sport.

(Glickman, 1998)

Reversal theory interpretation

Initially, Glickman experienced high felt arousal in the form of pre-race anxiety (telic–conformity). At the end of the race, after a tremendous physical effort, he experienced strong feelings of satisfaction from winning. He had achieved his goal and probably experienced high levels of hedonic tone in a telic–conformist state combination which probably also included the mastery and autic states.

Czech gold

At the 1998 Nagano Winter Olympics, the Czech Republic beat Russia 1–0 in the men's final to win its first gold medal in Olympic ice hockey. Czech coach Slavomir Lener said:

> We built a strong team around Hasek. . . . We had a great bunch of players working together as a team in this tournament. That's why we achieved the first-ever gold medal for Czech hockey.
>
> (Smaal, 1998)

Reversal theory interpretation

Lener's words suggest that the Czech team's strength was based on cooperation and identifying and working with each other towards a common purpose. These characteristics suggest a telic–alloic–sympathy state combination. However, in order for the team to be as successful as it was, during actual games on the ice the need to dominate and defeat the opposing team would have meant that the mastery and alloic states would probably have been prominent.

Cricket final

Summer 1999 saw the Cricket World Cup being held in England. England were eliminated in the early stages and the semi-finals saw Pakistan easily defeat New

Zealand. Australia defeated South Africa in the other semifinal when the two teams played to a tie and Australia went through to the final only on the basis of their superior standing in the 'Super Six' rankings. There had been some past bad feeling between the Pakistani and Australian players and it looked like being a tightly contested final at Lord's cricket ground in London. Wasim Akram, Pakistan's key player, said:

> When you're winning games so that you just have to stay in the competition, then you get a lot of stress, [said Akram, referring to Australia's string of seven must-win encounters]. If they're confident, then we're even more confident. We are mentally tougher than they are after what we've been through in the last two years . . . [and] we've prepared properly for the big game.
>
> ('More at stake', 1999)

Reversal theory interpretation

Pakistani captain Akram is alluding to the strong feelings of confidence and felt toughness in his team and the planning and work that has gone into its preparation for the final. These are defining features of the mastery and telic states.

Performance problems

In the 1999 Japan Open tennis tournament, Dutch player and top seed Richard Krajicek had some difficulty defeating David Prinosil of Germany, 6–4, 6–4. The second set was especially difficult and, even though he quickly went to a 5–1 lead, his big service was not working as well as usual. He had problems with the speed of the court and the speed of the ball through the air and admitted:

> Even at 5–1 up, I never felt I was in control of the match. . . . In general, I feel in control when I'm on hardcourts, but today I felt I couldn't put enough pressure on my second serve to come in and volley. So I felt I needed to get in some first serves, but that didn't happen either; then you feel you're not in control.
>
> (Varcoe, 1999)

Reversal theory interpretation

The autic and mastery states in reversal theory are important in sport and are often concerned with an athlete's desire to compete with and beat an opponent. However, they can also be important with regard to an athlete's technique or skills. Here Krajicek's desire for control in the match is probably related to the autic–mastery state combination and his inability under the particular court conditions and ball speed in this match to play at his best. He may have had difficulty in keeping the autic–mastery combination operative and salient under these match conditions. This would have led to feelings of poor felt transactional outcome and low levels of hedonic tone.

SECTION B

This section consists of extracts from an interview conducted by the author with Ross, a karate black belt. While the example quotations used above are useful aids in learning to recognise metamotivational states, interviews provide much more detailed information, in which the athlete's operative metamotivational states when performing and his or her metamotivational dominance can be studied in depth. Interspersed between interview extracts, the author's reversal theory interpretation of the athlete's comments is provided.

Ross, a 27-year-old Canadian from Montreal, is a shodan (1st Dan) or black belt in *Koshiki* karate (see Figure 2.1). *Koshiki* karate is an old, traditional form of karate which probably originates from Okinawa. The sport involves (a) forms of movements known as *kata*, (b) prearranged fighting using set patterns of movements, known as *yakusoka kumite*, (c) free fighting, known as *jiyu kumite*, and (d) meditation, known as *mokosou*. However, it also involves *shiai*, or full-contact fighting between athletes wearing protective gear over the head, chest and groin.

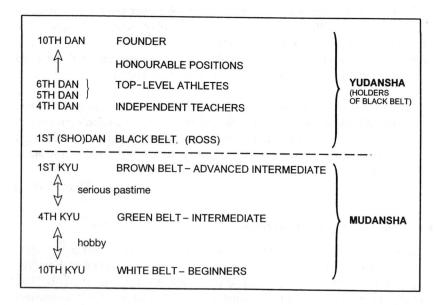

Figure 2.1 Koshiki karate levels.

Introduced to the sport when he was very young, Ross began his real involvement while he was at college. At high school, Ross was a C student academically and he had trouble getting accepted by a college. Eventually he was accepted at a college which had a policy of allowing its students a second chance to improve their academic standing. In his first year he really concentrated on his schooling, but in his second year, aged 19, he started karate again. By coincidence, the type of karate being taught at the college was *Koshiki* karate, the same type that he had studied when he was young. Also by coincidence, the karate teacher happened to be an English teacher who had attended high school with Ross. The interview was carried out with Ross some eight years later while he was taking a masters degree.

Ross, maybe you could tell me please how you first got involved in karate. How you first got interested?

OK. It's a rather interesting story in a way, because I started very young in judo. I was introduced to it by my father, who came from actually a very rough part of Montreal, and thought it would be good for his children. And I only took it very briefly. The instructor was a friend of our family. That was when I was very young. Then I came into contact with a friend of mine through school, who was studying the same karate that I do now and we were about 12 years old. And he went, and I used to go with him just because he was my best friend and he did it. I, again, was sort of interested in it for only a couple of months and dropped out. And I was a very meek child especially, so it was full-contact karate and it didn't very much appeal to me at the time. Then there is a big time span till I went through high school and into college.

Did you get involved in karate out of free choice, or were there friends or parents perhaps pushing you – you mentioned your dad, you mentioned this friend you had in your early school life?

When I was young my father brought us there, but very openly, just because we knew the teacher and we knew the family also. There was no obligation at all to stay, and in fact, you know, we had stopped. When I was at college I always remained intrigued at martial arts, and the side of martial arts which is the mental side of martial arts. And when I was at college I realised that it was a way to strengthen my mind, and so I opted to join 100 per cent on my own.

What was it that really got you interested in it? Was it this business of the mental side?

Yeah, there were really two reasons. The first one was again, at the time, being smaller and weighing less, not being as strong as a lot of the guys. You want to learn in order to protect yourself when you are also living in a big city. That was one aspect; that's a practical aspect. But the practical aspect for myself was never the overriding reason, that was sort of like a benefit certainly, but most importantly I always identified with the side of karate which is very much about the mental aspects. For some reason I always had an appreciation of that side. And I think I probably had some good examples of that earlier, for instance this man who was a friend of our family was very much like that. So when I was young, perhaps it stuck with me for some reason. Because many students just joined because they wanted to protect themselves, and they're not even aware of this other side of karate.

Reversal theory interpretation

Here it becomes apparent that Ross's motivation for taking up karate was likely to have been related to the mastery and telic states. He wanted to be able to defend himself against possible attack by bigger and stronger individuals and he was seriously interested in this form of karate because of the mental aspects associated with it.

Right, so you got seriously involved because of this spiritual side or . . . ?

Yeah, and I also felt at college, because I was going through this rationalisation of myself academically, and I said OK, now it's the time where I have to perform, I have to do the work. I am no longer in high school, and I can't screw around the rest of my life. I realised I had the need for, say, a pressure valve, or whatever. And I also realised that it was going to take time away from my studies, but, however, it helped me even to rationalise more my study time, even become a more effective student because it was taking time away, sort of counter-intuitive.

Reversal theory interpretation

Phrases like 'rationalisation of myself academically', 'have to do the work', 'I can't screw around the rest of my life' again point to a serious, planned, telic approach to his college work. However, he also realised the need to counterbalance the serious approach to work with some other activity such as karate which would act as 'a pressure valve' and might also indirectly help his studies.

It sounds as though you made a fairly serious decision; you thought about it carefully beforehand?

Yeah, I understood the karate studies as being something that you don't just walk in and walk out of classes like that. Because I also identified with the type of commitment that the teacher makes in that endeavour, to teach you. I didn't think it would be very worthy of someone just to walk in sort of on the fly and not take it seriously. So I wanted to, I imagine saying OK, for this scholastic year I'll go, I'll see what it is about but I'll give it my best effort.

Reversal theory interpretation

Ross is certain that, given the commitment of the karate teacher, a spontaneous or impulsive (paratelic) approach to karate is not something he could do. Karate requires serious commitment and cannot be entered into lightly. This is typical of telic–conformist-oriented behaviour. The respectful feeling he demonstrates towards his teacher also suggests alloic–mastery has a strong role to play here.

> *OK, tell me about the progression through the various belts and stages. How important is planning in all of that? Is the progress of stages very important – you know, by so and so I am going to be a brown belt, or I am going to be a black belt? Is that an important aspect of the whole sport?*

That's a very interesting question. In fact, I think ultimately the teachers want their students to have always in mind a progression, because you don't want students to get stagnated and that is one of the reasons why in the West we have this coloured belt system. In the East it really doesn't exist very much. However, you have to keep in mind always, OK, the next level, or gee, it would be nice if I could get my black belt or be a 2nd Dan. Like for myself right at the moment I think of 3rd Dan and I don't think of 2nd Dan. I think of achieving 3rd Dan, because then 2nd comes. But then again, you learn not to put your goal so high that you say I am going to be 5th Dan. And then you never achieve it and you get lost. So there is that, you learn that sort of through the other students of how to set your goals. And that is one of the practical things that you get out of karate. You learn how to goal-set your life. To a certain extent it is important, but the focus, the study of the karate is the technique of the concentration and of learning the new material is more important per se than achieving the different colours of belts, because that will come, as long as you concentrate yourself.

Reversal theory interpretation

Karate requires goal setting and step-by-step progress, thus providing Ross with satisfaction of goal achievement associated with the telic state. It is also future oriented in that the extrinsic rewards of achieving the different ability levels come later. By investing effort now in hard training, the next level can be achieved easily in the future. Again, this is indicative of telic-oriented behaviour also strongly linked to the mastery state.

> *OK, good. Why do you think you yourself were successful at karate and what made you continue to participate?*

One reason certainly is having the focus to give it the time that is required. Because there is the technical aspect of the sport which you have to master to a certain degree, which takes time, like any sport. And there is also the mental side, again the philosophical side is very difficult for students in martial arts, especially one that is full contact, even though we have a safety gear system where you really don't get hurt, but it is sort of rough on the body to a certain extent that, if you practise for years, one of the things that keeps you going is the philosophy of karate, why you are there. If you don't have that, it is very difficult to keep going. I was able to identify early with that side of the study, and that helped me to go on, and I think also getting deeply into my own psyche? I tend to think often of my childhood, when I was very meek and mild, as I put it, and when I think of that, that spurs me on to continue to progress, to improve, because it is a good reflection for me, to say 'look what you have achieved', and that spurs me on to continue. Because we have a lot of examples in karate where people start, they have a natural ability for the sport, as in any sport you can imagine, they're there for a couple of years and then you don't see them any more. And they are not willing to make the commitment to study very diligently to get the black belt. And everything has come easy for them and when it starts coming hard for them then they drop out. I was always good at karate, but never so good that it came so easy. Every time I practised I had to concentrate very much to get the movements and also, I mentioned often the karate philosophy, one of the philosophies which gets into Zen is the search for perfection as the Japanese put it. And it is not the attainment of the goal, but it is the process which is most important. So in our studies really we try to teach the students by example and by telling them straight out that, you know, worry about getting there and not being there. Don't worry about the end, but worry about the process.

Reversal theory interpretation

From this previous paragraph and what has gone before, it is now possible to piece together an analysis of Ross's primary motivation for karate in terms of a state combination. Reversal theorists would recognise that Ross's description of the hard, diligent, constant practice necessary for karate is associated with a state combination of telic–autic–mastery. Incidentally, Ross mentions the important influence of Zen in the philosophy associated with karate. Fontana (1991) has argued that the Zen state of mind that is sought in karate and some other sports occurs in the paratelic state. What Ross said about concentrating on the process (paratelic) rather than the end (telic) seems to support Fontana's view, but also appears to contradict what Ross says earlier in the piece above. By working hard at practising kata in the telic state, it may be that as the athlete becomes totally concentrated and absorbed in the activity, a reversal from the telic to the paratelic state takes place, allowing the athlete to achieve the so-called Zen state.

When you say 'the search for perfection', do you mean perfection in the movements themselves?

Yeah, you would make that analogous to the movements because we have a *kata* which is a stream of movements that you are supposed to learn one after the other, say thirty movements put together, almost similar to a ballet, for instance. You try and execute your techniques perfectly, as crisp as possible, one after the other with the proper timing and grace, if you will. That you are trying to do, those are the physical technical movements. And then behind that, in order to be able to do that extremely well, you have to have a perfection of your mind, the clarity of the mind, and a focus of the mind. So that is what the perfection is. However, the Japanese are well aware that perfection is something that is metaphysical, you can never attain perfection, so it is the search for it. And that also tells you at square one you are never going to arrive there. So, since you have already the assumption that you are never going to be a perfect karate player, then you say OK, well, under that assumption then my dedication to do karate is exactly that. I don't get anything, there is no present at the end. You do it because you do karate.

These sets of exercises, these strings of thirty exercises, who decides what they are, are they set exercises?

Yeah. These have been passed down since time immemorial almost, some come from China, some are made in Japan, and some are being formed as we speak. So they're passed on. For instance, the school of ours which is in Japan are practising the same thing that we would be practising, and there you learn one *kata* at each level, so right at the moment I know say ten, eleven *kata*, which is difficult because then you are talking about three to four hundred movements. They are all of various lengths and you've got to keep practising or you would lose them, naturally. When you get to black belt level, one of the hard parts is you're required to learn new material; however, you have a lot of time to spend just to keep your old material still at hand.

So the whole thing is that you have to diligently follow these movements every time you practise?

Yeah, there are really three focuses of karate training. There is that focus which is *kata*, there is *kumite*, which is called prearranged fighting, which is where you and I square off against each other. However, you know what I am doing as an offensive move, and I know what you're doing as a defensive move. And you probably have say ten movements, I have ten movements, and then we perform them in concert. We never hit each other, we're always missing, because since you know my attack you can defend properly. But this forces you to do the timing and the distance of your movements to execute them better. So it is a different way of teaching the movements, it's more dynamic. Again, you would have these movements which are shorter in total, say ten movements together, you would learn two of these *kumite* at each level, approximately. And then, for instance, to give you an idea of the black belt exam, everything you've learned before your black belt exam you have to repeat in your examination. So you have your ten or eleven *kata* and you have your ten *kumite* that you have to perform. Then there is actually the *shiai*, which is the fighting. Which doesn't take on in our style very much importance; it gets more important as you get higher and higher because your technical ability is becoming greater. However, I think it is no more than 30 per cent of the time. So a couple of focuses there.

Reversal theory interpretation

The paragraphs immediately above emphasise the importance of sticking to the established protocol during the exercises and the prearranged fighting. The conformist state can be added to the other three to make a four-way combination of telic–conformist–autic–mastery.

Can you describe your feelings when you're actually in one of these – I have forgotten the technical word – fights with somebody else, these rehearsed fights?

Right. There is *kumite*, which is the prearranged fighting; however, I think maybe a question that is similar to that is, we also, when we're going to train in our school, there's say thirty other students with us that I have now spent five or six years minimum with, and there's the new students. And we practise together because there is a lot of just individual movements that our teacher likes us to learn. And then there are different groups in the class practising different *kata*. Now, you go there, and you're in the class, and you have your friends with you which helps to spur you on. Now, one of the things that people in the West sort of misunderstand about karate is, it is an individual sport and it is also a group sport. OK, it is individual because it is sort of like in a thorough mind that you have to be self-reliant, because when it comes to the practicality of martial arts of combat you are the only one who is there to protect yourself, in that particular eventuality. However, the class itself is structured along Japanese society where everybody is equal, no matter what level they're at. And no one is more important than the other. OK. And also the highest black belt is concerned about the lowest white belt and vice versa. So it's very much a community feeling that everybody helps each other to pass the levels also. So none is left on their own, to say, you have a black belt exam to pass, or you have a green belt exam to pass in two weeks, go and do it. Everybody is concerned that they will successfully pass their examination. From that point, that is a great advantage for me, because that gives you a feeling, a sense of community with everyone after so many years of practising with them. A good school will tend to be a good family also.

Reversal theory interpretation

Ross's reply is important because, although the autic and mastery states have been to the forefront in some of Ross's other comments, here it can be seen that the alloic and sympathy states also have a role to play in karate and that reversals to and from these states also take place. Experience in these states is exemplified by the phrases 'a sense of community with everyone' and 'the highest black belt is concerned about the lowest white belt and vice versa'.

So karate is really a fundamental element in your lifestyle?

Yes, and the way I think also.

Can you expand on that a little bit?

Well certainly. I was mentioning before the individualism of karate that's definitely something that I've – often, maybe too much? [laughs]. There's that then, the philosophy of karate – that karate itself is a process, is analogous to life, that life is a process. You have to learn to attack in stages. You have to learn also to accept things that come, and continue on and look on to the next thing. And live each day, if you will, as best as you can and to get as much out of it as you can. And we learn that when you get something that seems like it is insurmountable, that it really isn't, that you have to just learn to take one step at a time, like a voyage of a thousand miles begins with a first step. And I very much learned that lesson of life, so whereas, you know, I have noticed with my friends from high school that I still talk with, and my girlfriend at home, you know the philosophies that we have about just doing things is completely different. Whereas you see people who can get overwhelmed by things. That you realise that everything is an aggregate of its ingredients and if you just attack one step at a time that sooner or later you reach the end. So that's something that spurs me on.

Reversal theory interpretation

It is obvious that for Ross, karate is more than just a sport. He relates the philosophy of karate to his own philosophy of life. In fact, the two seem to be so intertwined that his involvement in karate is just an extension of his lifestyle. Therefore, if we go beyond the metamotivational state level of analysis, Ross is a telic-dominant athlete and it is very likely that he is also conformity, autic and mastery dominant. This is apparent from his whole approach to work and study as well as his approach to karate.

CLOSING COMMENTS

With practice and some experience it becomes possible to analyse what athletes say in terms of reversal theory metamotivational states and dominance. Such an analysis, founded on a systematic theoretical base, can provide the sport psychologist with added insight into the motivation, personality and emotional experience of the athlete. There are many different examples included in this chapter which have been interpreted in terms of the different states and state combinations available in the theory. However, some combinations are less common in sport than others and in some cases it is difficult to find meaningful examples. In other words, reversal theory is not completely exhausted by sport.

A number of reversal theory tools are available for the sport psychologist to use with athletes. These consist of different types of psychological scales and inventories which can be used to measure operative metamotivational states and dominance. Some details and examples of how the measures can be used to assist in metamotivational identification are provided in the next chapter.

SUGGESTED FURTHER READING

Kerr, J. H. (ed.) (1999) *Experiencing Sport: Reversal Theory*, Chichester: Wiley.
Wilson, G. V. and Kerr, J. H. (1999) 'Affective responses to success and failure: a study of winning and losing in competitive rugby', *Personality and Individual Differences* 27: 85–99.
Males, J. R., Kerr, J. H. and Gerkovich, M. (1998) 'Metamotivational states during canoe slalom competition: a qualitative analysis using reversal theory', *Journal of Applied Sport Psychology* 10: 184–200.

FOR DISCUSSION

Consider the following examples of athlete quotations. Attempt to make your own reversal theory interpretation of the material in each quotation, trying to answer the following three questions in each case:

1   Which metamotivational state or state combination was likely to have been operative in each example?
2   Which motivational variables (e.g. felt arousal) were likely to have been involved?
3   Can any of reversal theory's sixteen primary emotions be identified?

Check your interpretation against the author's reversal theory interpretation at the end of this chapter.

1   Olympic veteran

Not many athletes can claim to be a veteran of five Olympic teams. However, 33-year-old 400 and 800 metre runner Charmain Crooks is one who can, and this is why she was chosen to be the flagbearer leading the Canadian contingent during the opening ceremonies of the Twenty-sixth Summer Olympic Games. After the announcement at the Canadian Olympic Association's official reception, Crooks said:

> In 1984, the first Olympics I competed in, I was really young and I was very excited. . . . There was so much going on and I was a little overwhelmed, I think. But I went in and did very well. Those games were also in the United States and things were very familiar. Things here in Atlanta are also pretty similar to home so I feel very comfortable being here. But that excitement, I guess I do feel a little bit the way I felt in 1984, just as excited.
>
> ('Olympic veteran', 1996)

2   Place kicker in rugby

Paul Grayson, Northampton and England rugby player, usually has the responsibility for place-kicking. He scored the most points in the 1997 and 1998 Five Nations championships for England. In an article for *Rugby World* magazine he explained his mental approach to consistent goal-kicking:

> There are occasions when the winning points in the match are down to me. When I am facing the posts for a conversion of penalty I don't think about missing. It doesn't enter my head. I am there to score the goal and make the points. . . .
>
> My mental focus comes from self belief. The knowledge that I can do what I have to do. As soon as you let doubt creep in you may as well give up. You have to set yourself goals and then analyse your mental approach as well as your physical results.
>
> (Ford, 1998)

3   Return from injury

At the February 1998 BUPA Grand Prix track and field athletics indoor meet in Birmingham, US triple Olympic gold medalist Gail Devers won the women's 60 metre sprint. She was returning after a very long period out of the action with an Achilles tendon injury. Her winning time of 7.04 seconds was the fastest for the season until then. The 1992 and 1996 Olympic 100 metre winner said:

I'm happy to get through that and that I'm healthy. . . . I haven't run for aeons and I'm very excited to be here and winning. Now I can run some more indoor races and get ready for the outdoor season.

('Gebrselassie', 1998)

4 Wimbledon semifinals

At Wimbledon in July 1996, Steffi Graf reached the semifinals. Graf had a chance to win for the seventh time in the Wimbledon women's singles championship. A win would have brought her into second place behind Margaret Court, who achieved twenty-four grand slam titles. Graf pointed out that:

I am happy if I win the match and happier if I play well. That's more important to me than records. Maybe at the end of my career that's something I can look back on and be proud of, but not right now.

('Date tops Pierce', 1996)

5 Formula One car racing

Canadian Jacques Villeneuve, who was one of the favourites to win the 1997 Formula One car-racing title, got himself into trouble in February of that year when he said:

I think they've gone a bit overboard on safety. . . . The sport is safe enough and I would like to see a little more excitement.

('Villeneuve', 1997)

6 Giants quarterback

San Francisco Giants quarterback Steve Young, one of the best passers in the National Football League, talked to Bruce Weber for *Coach and Athletic Director* magazine. Among the many comments he made were these:

Fear is a fantastic motivator. Fear of failure, fear of not getting the job done, fear of not being able to succeed – it's a tremendous motivator. It's not necessarily negative.

I'm still motivated by the fear of not accomplishing what I know I can, to turn away from what I know I can do. It has been a mark of my whole career that I keep at it. There's always possible improvement out there. There are things that I'll fail miserably at for a long time. So I just keep at it until I get there. Those moments when you actually achieve what you've always thought that you couldn't do are maybe the greatest moments in your career.

(Weber, 1998)

7 Stanley Cup hockey final

In ice hockey, the final of the Stanley Cup is often a thriller, but it would be hard to beat the 1999 final between the Dallas Stars and the Buffalo Sabres. The controversial winning goal came in the third period of overtime and was scored by Brett Hull. Members of the Sabres team argued that Hull's left skate was in the crease as he scored. However, the goal was allowed to stand, giving Dallas a 2–1 win. Bobby, Brett's father, had previously won a National Hockey League title with Chicago in 1961 and Brett said:

> It is unbelievable starting out as a kid growing up in that shadow and finally making a niche for myself. . . . This finally completes the cycle. I hope someday my son or grand kids can do it.

Ken Hitchcock, coach of the Dallas Stars, also said:

> It was really worth it. . . . It was such an endurance test. I'm proud of the team. They reached every goal we set. It was unbelievable.
>
> ('Stars claim Cup', 1999)

8 Rain at Wimbledon tennis

It rained during the early stages of the 1997 Wimbledon tennis tournament. Tournament organisers had to use the middle Sunday, normally a free day, to catch up with delayed matches. One of those matches involved English player Tim Henman against Dutchman Paul Haarhuis on the Centre Court. Thousands of fans had queued, some through the night, in order to get seats for the extra day's play. During his five-set victory the crowd got behind Henman, helping him to avoid defeat when, at one stage, Haarhuis held match point at 5–4. Henman, talking later about the supportive fans, said:

> From the word go, it was something I'd never experienced before. . . . The noise was just a totally different level. I always have great support here, but in the situation of a middle Sunday that crowd played a huge part in the match. . . . It gives you an amazing sort of buzz.
>
> ('Hen-mania hits Wimbledon', 1997)

In the next round, Henman defeated Richard Krajicek, another Dutchman, but, with everything going to plan, his performance slumped dramatically and he lost to Michael Stich of Germany. In an exclusive interview he described the match as 'probably my worst experience on a tennis court' and went on to explain:

Today I didn't just let myself down. I earned myself a debt to the thousands of people who have given me the best support any British sportsman could ever ask for. But to all those who have queued night after night on the pavements of Wimbledon, or even the millions who have willed me on from in front of their television sets, I promise one thing: I will be back, and one day I will win this title for them.

('I owe you', 1997)

9 Ice hockey injury

Andreas Dackell, right wing with the Ottawa Senators ice hockey team, was badly injured in a game with the Flyers. Eric Lindros body-checked Andreas after he chased a puck into the left corner. It was a very hard but fair check, which drove Andreas into the glass wall face first and resulted in his being stretchered off the ice suffering from concussion and bleeding from severe lacerations caused by his helmet visor. Later, thirty stitches were needed to sew up the cuts. Eric Lindros was quoted after the game as saying:

I felt horrible. No one likes to see that. . . . I just went in to finish my check and he ducked and twisted. I'm not really sure what happened to him or how he got hurt.

('Dackell out', 1998)

FOR DISCUSSION REVISITED

Below is the author's reversal theory interpretation of the athlete quotes found in the previous section.

1 What Crooks is referring to here is what reversal theorists would recognise as high felt arousal feelings of excitement in a paratelic–conformist state combination.

2 From Grayson's remarks, it seems likely that the telic–autic–mastery meta-motivational state combination is operative when he is place-kicking in rugby. The general attitude conveyed in the first quoted paragraph, and cues such as *goals*, *analyse* and *self-belief* in the second, lead to this assessment.

3 Devers' excitement suggests high felt arousal in a paratelic–conformist state combination. After a long period of telic-oriented injury rehabilitation, it may be that after this race, which she came through without further injury, she was excited and grateful. These feelings probably indicate that, post-race, the paratelic state was probably operative in combination with the autic and sympathy states.

4   Graf's comments mark the greater immediate importance to her of winning and playing well as compared with achieving records. In reversal theory terms, this indicates the salience of the mastery over the telic and other states. At this time, mastery over opponents and technique form the basis of her pleasant feelings of high felt transactional gain. This may change later when her playing career is over and pleasant feelings of pride (autic–mastery) may become associated with her records. In reversal theory terms, for Graf, having the mastery state operative when playing tennis is of prime importance.

5   Reversal theory sport research has shown that athletes participating in high-risk sports score low on the arousal-avoidance scale of the TDS (Kerr, 1991), indicating that they tend to be sensation-oriented arousal seekers. Here, Villeneuve adds to that evidence, making a plea for less safety and more high-arousal paratelic experiences.

6   Telic–conformist fear or anxiety, tied in with telic-oriented goal achievement, is evident from Young's interview comments, especially the phrase 'I keep at it'. However, his 'fear' is also about losing in terms of felt transactional outcome in his interactions with others. Also, at the end of the quoted remarks he alludes to elements of successful performance which are typical of the autic–mastery state combination.

7   Implicit in Hull's and obvious in Coach Hitchcock's comments are their feelings of pride and satisfaction. In Hull's case these feelings arise from his personal satisfaction in being able to achieve what his father had achieved; in Hitchcock's case from his team's determination and goal achievement. Pride is an autic–mastery emotion and goal achievement is associated with the telic state. Hence, the source of these feelings is likely to be a metamotivational state combination of telic–autic–mastery.

8   In the first match, Henman related strongly to the support from the crowd and was grateful to them. In terms of felt transactional outcome, he experienced pleasant feelings of net gain in an autic–sympathy state combination. Later in the tournament, when he lost, he appears to have felt unpleasant shame and an overall sense of net loss in an alloic–mastery state combination.

9   Transactional emotions are involved here and the experience of negative hedonic tone and overall feelings of net loss. It was a bad injury caused by a very hard, but fair, body-check. Even though there is no evidence that Lindros intended to injure Dackell, he may have been experiencing some feelings of shame (alloic–mastery) or guilt (alloic–sympathy) from the outcome.

Chapter 3

Measuring athletes' states and dominance

MEASURING STATES

The use of short 'state-type' questionnaires and checklists is now very common in psychology. They have proved especially useful in allowing an individual's mental state, or changes in mental state, to be monitored in particular situations and over time. Sport psychologists, following the trend in other areas of psychology, have been using state measures for well over ten years in research and practice. In some cases, sport psychologists have borrowed state measures already being used in other areas of psychology (e.g. the State–Trait Anxiety Inventory; Spielberger *et al.*, 1970), adapting them for use in sport (e.g. the Sport Competition Anxiety Test; Martens, 1977). In other cases, specially designed sport-specific measures have been utilised (e.g. the Sport Orientation Questionnaire; Gill and Deeter, 1988, or the Running Addiction Questionnaire; Chapman and De Castro, 1990). Athletes have generally been cooperative and willing to complete state measures as long as they are short and do not intrude on performance.

In reversal theory sport research and practice, measures developed for general psychological use have been used in sport situations and a custom-designed sport-specific measure has recently become available. Before the development of this new measure, the State of Mind Indicator for Athletes (SOMIFA; Kerr and Apter, 1999), the Telic State Measure (TSM; e.g. Svebak and Murgatroyd, 1985) was the instrument of choice for monitoring operative metamotivational state and felt arousal levels in athletes. Both are easily administered short state-type scales which can be completed in a few minutes, thus lending themselves to repeated measurement if desired (e.g. pre- and post-competition). The SOMIFA has some advantages over the TSM and these will be pointed out below. First, though, let us examine the TSM and some of the contexts in which it has successfully been used.

Telic State Measure (TSM)

The earliest published use of the TSM was in psychophysiological work carried out by Sven Svebak and his colleagues in Bergen, Norway (Svebak *et al.*, 1982). However, it was in a later publication (Svebak and Murgatroyd, 1985), in which the authors reported a multimethod validation of reversal theory constructs (especially metamotivational dominance), that the real potential of the TSM for empirical work could be seen. Svebak and Murgatroyd (1985) used a combination of quantitative and qualitative methods in their research. The TSM was used together with interviews to provide additional information about the differences in operative metamotivational state in extreme telic- and paratelic-dominant individuals during a psychophysiological experiment examining muscle tension patterns.

Contemporary versions of the TSM consist of five items, each with a six-point rating scale with defining adjectives at each end. The items include (1) serious–playful, (2) preferred planned–preferred spontaneous, (3) low felt arousal–high felt arousal, (4) preferred low arousal–preferred high arousal, (5) low effort–high effort. Item (5), the investment of effort in a task (low effort–high effort), is completed only after a task and was a later addition to the TSM. A sixth item, arousal discrepancy, is computed by subtracting the score for item (3) (felt arousal) from the score for item (4) (preferred arousal) (see Figure 3.1). Note that on items (1) and (2), low scores (1–3) are taken to indicate the telic state and high scores (4–6) the paratelic state. Subjects should be made familiar with the measure prior to its use and should be given instructions as to how to respond to the items (for example, reporting how they feel at the time of completion).

In the sport context, the TSM has been used, for example, to measure psychological responses to winning and losing in squash (Cox and Kerr, 1989, 1990) and in rugby (Kerr and van Schaik, 1995). It has also been used to identify reversals in metamotivational state induced by long-distance running (Kerr and Vlaswinkel, 1993) and in a study examining running intensity and metamotivational state and arousal (Kerr and van den Wollenberg, 1997). Kerr and Tacon (1999) used the TSM to investigate metamotivational state and arousal levels in recreational badminton. Further information on the TSM and its use in sport research can be found in Kerr (1997). Below is an illustration of how the TSM can be used in practice.

Anna: field hocky umpire

Anna is a 34-year-old Dutch field hockey umpire. She had pursued a successful career as a top-level hockey player until the age of 26, when she stopped to concentrate on her developing career as an umpire. She is now an international-level umpire. She agreed to complete a Dutch version of the TSM at half-time during two hockey matches. One was a closely contested, difficult-to-umpire national championship match, and the other was an easy-to-referee lower-level match. Figure 3.2 shows a graphical representation of Anna's scores during the two matches. Straightforward visual comparison (no statistical analysis has been carried out) suggests that she was more serious and more planning oriented (i.e., more telic) during the closely contested, difficult-to-umpire national championship match than during the easy match. Also, her felt arousal level was considerably lower

Name: Gender: M/F   Age: 21

INSTRUCTIONS

Please rate your feelings at this moment in terms of the five following rating scales.
Do this by circling a number.

1.   Estimate here how playful or serious you feel.

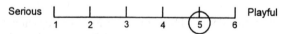

2.   Estimate here how far you would prefer to plan ahead or to be spontaneous.

3.   Estimate here how aroused ('worked up') you actually feel.

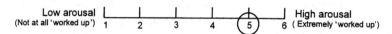

4.   Estimate here the level of arousal (how 'worked up') you would like to feel.

5.   Estimate here how much effort you invested in the task.

Figure 3.1 A copy of the TSM completed by a recreational badminton player just prior
to playing (from Kerr and Tacon, 1999).

during the easy match, but she would have preferred to have been more aroused.
Here there was a discrepancy between her felt and preferred levels of arousal. As
a result, she may have been experiencing some paratelic tension stress during this
lower-level game. By contrast, in the difficult game, her levels of felt and preferred
arousal were equal and there was no arousal discrepancy and therefore no tension
stress. However, note that the level of effort she had to put into the difficult game
was higher than that required for the easy game. The TSM, used in this way, can
give a quick and useful insight into the experiences of a sport participant, in this
case a hockey umpire, during a match. It can be used equally effectively with
performing athletes.

Two other reversal theory state measures do exist, but these have not been widely
used in sport research. The Somatic State Questionnaire (SSQ; Cook, Gerkovich
et al., 1993) measures whether a person is in the telic or paratelic and negativistic or conformist metamotivational states, as well as arousal preference. The

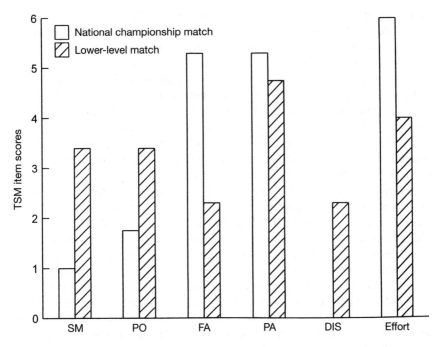

Figure 3.2 An umpire's contrasting TSM item scores when officiating at a closely contested, difficult-to-umpire national championship match and a lower-level, easy-to-umpire match.

Telic/Paratelic State Instrument (T/PSI; Calhoun, 1995; Calhoun and O'Connell, 1995) was also designed to measure whether a person was in the telic or paratelic state and the level of arousal. Cogan and Brown (1998) did include the T/PSI in their study of metamotivational dominance, states and injuries in risk and safe sports.

The State of Mind Indicator for Athletes (SOMIFA)

The SOMIFA (Kerr and Apter, 1999) was custom designed for use in sport and has several advantages when compared to the TSM. First, it covers all four pairs of metamotivational states, whereas the TSM deals only with the telic and paratelic pair. Second, athletes make a simple choice between partner metamotivational states by indicating which one of two statements (one for each state in four sets of statements) best represents their state of mind during performance. This has an advantage over the TSM in that athletes do not have to indicate, for example, how serious or playful they are feeling along a dimension from 1 to 6. With the range of scores on the serious–playful dimension, it has sometimes proved difficult to decide whether athletes indicating the middle scores on the dimension (i.e., 3 or

4) were in the telic or the paratelic state. Third, on the SOMIFA, athletes are asked to indicate which statement, of the four statements chosen, they were most aware of during performance. This allows the researcher to infer which metamotivational state was salient during performance. Fourth, the felt arousal and preferred arousal items from the TSM have been divided into three different dimensions of arousal (calm–worked up, sleepy–wide awake, fatigued–energetic) to better reflect reversal theory's theoretical distinction between different forms of arousal. Previous reversal theory sport research has shown that discrepancies between levels of felt and preferred arousal were important in distinguishing between successful performance and unsuccessful performance in athletes (e.g. Males and Kerr, 1996; Cox and Kerr, 1989). Fifth, the final item on the SOMIFA is a dimension assessing the athlete's perception of how well they thought they had performed. This type of item addressing self-perception of performance had not been included in previous research using the TSM, and its inclusion in the SOMIFA provides additional information about the athlete's experience. More information on the development of the SOMIFA can be found in Kerr (1999), and two examples of the SOMIFA completed by athletes are shown in Figures 3.3A and 3.3B.

Figure 3.3A shows the SOMIFA completed by a 30-year-old male 5,000 metre track-and-field athlete who had been runner-up in a recent world championship. It was completed on a 'one-to-one' researcher/athlete basis after a European series 5,000 metre race which he won. It is interesting to note that he marked the telic, negativistic, mastery and alloic responses, and he was most aware of the need to achieve something important (that is, the telic state was salient). Therefore, his operative state combination during the race was one of telic–negativistic–alloic – mastery. There was no discrepancy in any of the arousal dimensions between felt and preferred arousal, suggesting that he achieved the levels of arousal that he desired for performance. He also rated his own performance highly in a race which he won.

Figure 3.3B shows the SOMIFA completed by a 25-year-old male track-and-field sprinter, who at the time was the third fastest man in the world with a time of 9.91 seconds for the 100 metres. Again, it was completed on a 'one-to-one' researcher/athlete basis post-race at the same European series meet. The sprinter's responses (telic, conformist, mastery, autic) show some differences from those of the 5,000 metre runner, and he also indicated that he was most aware of being tough and dominating over his opponents during performance (that is, the mastery state rather than the telic state was salient). His operative state combination during the race was one of telic–conformist–autic–mastery. There was a discrepancy between felt and preferred arousal on all three arousal dimensions, indicating that the sprinter felt that he was not worked up, wide awake and energetic enough during the event. He scored his own performance as above average, coming in sixth in a time of 10.06 seconds.

As shown in Figures 3.3A and 3.3B, the SOMIFA instructions ask the athlete to answer the questions about his or her state of mind during the preceding performance. The instructions can, of course, be altered to 'tap into' an athlete's state of mind pre-competition, or even during performance in some sports where breaks in performance occur. In this way, the SOMIFA becomes a valuable tool to the sport psychologist, one which can, if used repeatedly for a period, be used to build up a profile (e.g. Terry, 1995) of the athlete's most desired, or optimal, state of mind when competing. Subsequently, it can be used to pinpoint occasions when the athlete's operative states differ, perhaps as a result of some performance-related problem, from those identified as optimal for competition. This knowledge would allow the sport psychologist and athlete, or the athlete him or herself, if well versed in reversal theory and psychological techniques, to undertake a cognitive intervention strategy if required.

The Tension and Effort Stress Inventory (TESI)

Operative metamotivational states can also be determined indirectly using the TESI (Svebak, 1993; Svebak *et al.*, 1991). It has the added advantage of being able to measure tension stress, effort stress, and the strength of any of reversal theory's sixteen primary emotions that an athlete may be experiencing. It was used initially to predict academic performance (Svebak, 1997) and to identify psychological factors in the aetiology of back pain (Svebak *et al.*, 1991).

The TESI is relatively short, with a total of twenty individual response items to which athletes respond by circling the appropriate figure on a scale of 1 to 7 ranging from 'not at all' to 'very much'. The pleasant and unpleasant somatic and transactional emotions comprise sixteen of the twenty response items, i.e. somatic emotions – relaxation, excitement, placidity, provocativeness (pleasant); anxiety, anger, boredom, sullenness (unpleasant); transactional emotions – pride, gratitude, modesty, virtue (pleasant); humiliation, resentment, shame, guilt (unpleasant). Overall scores for total pleasant and unpleasant emotions, which reflect overall hedonic tone, are usually computed, although individual emotions can be considered independently. The emotion items are preceded by the remaining four items, which are concerned with tension stress arising from situational factors and bodily factors, and the effort stress needed to cope with the effects of the two forms of tension stress. In the introductory instructions at the top of the TESI, the time period in question can be specified (e.g. 'over the past thirty days', 'over the past week' or 'right now' (TESI state version)).

The TESI has been used in sport research to examine changes in stress and emotion in sport (e.g. Kerr and Svebak, 1994; Males and Kerr, 1996; Wilson and Kerr, 1999). For example, Wilson and Kerr (1999) used the TESI in their study of winning and losing in rugby, and Wilson (1999) showed how it is possible to determine which metamotivational states were operative from the emotions the rugby players indicated that they had experienced. The results of this particular study showed that both winners and losers exhibited similar pre-game emotions. These were the pleasant emotions excitement, provocativeness and pride, arising from state combinations of paratelic–conformity, paratelic–negativism and autic–mastery, respectively. However, important post-game differences between

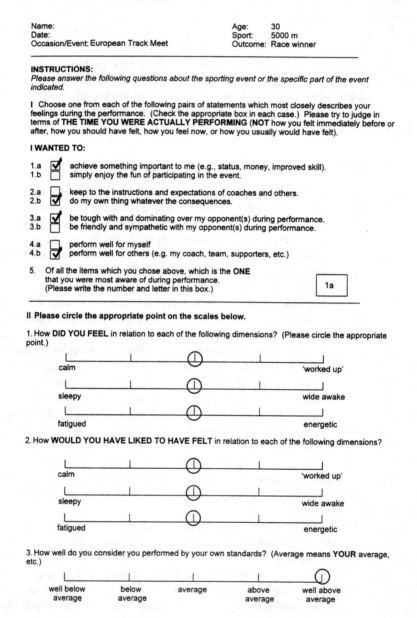

Name: Age: 30
Date: Sport: 5000 m
Occasion/Event: European Track Meet   Outcome: Race winner

INSTRUCTIONS:
Please answer the following questions about the sporting event or the specific part of the event indicated.

I Choose one from each of the following pairs of statements which most closely describes your feelings during the performance. (Check the appropriate box in each case.) Please try to judge in terms of **THE TIME YOU WERE ACTUALLY PERFORMING (NOT** how you felt immediately before or after, how you should have felt, how you feel now, or how you usually would have felt).

I WANTED TO:

1.a ☑ achieve something important to me (e.g., status, money, improved skill).
1.b ☐ simply enjoy the fun of participating in the event.

2.a ☐ keep to the instructions and expectations of coaches and others.
2.b ☑ do my own thing whatever the consequences.

3.a ☑ be tough with and dominating over my opponent(s) during performance.
3.b ☐ be friendly and sympathetic with my opponent(s) during performance.

4.a ☐ perform well for myself
4.b ☑ perform well for others (e.g. my coach, team, supporters, etc.)

5. Of all the items which you chose above, which is the **ONE** that you were most aware of during performance. (Please write the number and letter in this box.) | 1a |

II Please circle the appropriate point on the scales below.

1. How **DID YOU FEEL** in relation to each of the following dimensions? (Please circle the appropriate point.)

calm ————————ⓘ———————— 'worked up'

sleepy ————————ⓘ———————— wide awake

fatigued ———————ⓘ———————— energetic

2. How **WOULD YOU HAVE LIKED TO HAVE FELT** in relation to each of the following dimensions?

calm ————————ⓘ———————— 'worked up'

sleepy ————————ⓘ———————— wide awake

fatigued ————————ⓘ———————— energetic

3. How well do you consider you performed by your own standards? (Average means **YOUR** average, etc.)

well below   below   average   above   well above
 average   average   average   average

Figure 3.3A A copy of the SOMIFA completed post-race by an elite 5,000 metre runner.

Name:

Date:

Occasion/Event: European Track Meet

Age: 25

Sport: 100 m

Outcome: 6th place

INSTRUCTIONS:

Please answer the following questions about the sporting event or the specific part of the event indicated.

I Choose one from each of the following pairs of statements which most closely describes your feelings during the performance. (Check the appropriate box in each case.) Please try to judge in terms of **THE TIME YOU WERE ACTUALLY PERFORMING (NOT** how you felt immediately before or after, how you should have felt, how you feel now, or how you usually would have felt).

I WANTED TO:

1.a ☑ achieve something important to me (e.g., status, money, improved skill).

1.b ☐ simply enjoy the fun of participating in the event.

2.a ☑ keep to the instructions and expectations of coaches and others.

2.b ☐ do my own thing whatever the consequences.

3.a ☑ be tough with and dominating over my opponent(s) during performance.

3.b ☐ be friendly and sympathetic with my opponent(s) during performance.

4.a ☑ perform well for myself

4.b ☐ perform well for others (e.g. my coach, team, supporters, etc.)

5. Of all the items which you chose above, which is the **ONE** that you were most aware of during performance. (Please write the number and letter in this box.)

3a

II Please circle the appropriate point on the scales below.

1. How **DID YOU FEEL** in relation to each of the following dimensions? (Please circle the appropriate point.)

calm ⸺⊙⸺ 'worked up'

sleepy ⸺⊙⸺ wide awake

fatigued ⸺⊙⸺ energetic

2. How **WOULD YOU HAVE LIKED TO HAVE FELT** in relation to each of the following dimensions?

calm ⸺⊙⸺ 'worked up'

sleepy ⸺⊙⸺ wide awake

fatigued ⸺⊙⸺ energetic

3. How well do you consider you performed by your own standards? (Average means **YOUR** average, etc.)

well below average	below average	average	above average	well above average

Figure 3.3B A copy of the SOMIFA completed post-race by an elite male sprinter.

winners and losers were identified. Winning was a pleasant experience producing relaxation, excitement (reduced from pre-game levels), gratitude, virtue and pride (reduced from pre-game levels), indicating that state combinations of telic–conformity, paratelic–conformity, autic–sympathy, alloic–sympathy and autic–mastery, respectively, were operative among the different players. Losing produced the unpleasant emotions anger and sullenness, arising from telic and paratelic–negativism, and humiliation, shame and resentment, arising from autic–mastery, alloic–mastery and autic–sympathy state combinations. Decreases in pride and virtue also took place with losing.

The TESI can also be used in the type of quantitative diary methodology advocated by Clough *et al.* (1996). This methodology can provide in-depth information about an athlete's pattern of emotions and stress mapped over a period of days. The example of Yoko, a 27-year-old Japanese former world champion who underwent a period of sport injury rehabilitation, is described next, to illustrate how this can be carried out using the TESI. In this example, raw scores have been used, but, if desired, standardised scores can be computed (e.g. z-scores; Clough *et al.*, 1996).

Yoko: injured athlete in rehabilitation

While competing in the world championships, Yoko ruptured the anterior cruciate ligament in her left knee and medical specialists advised her to have surgery to repair the damage. Yoko spent a total of sixty days in hospital to have the operation and undergo post-operative rehabilitation work to strengthen her knee. After the operation, her time in hospital could be divided into periods which corresponded to progressive stages in her rehabilitation after the operation (see Table 3.1).

Table 3.1 Post-operative rehabilitation

Stage 1	Leg encased in a plaster cast, movement restricted to using a wheelchair.
Stage 2	Plaster cast removed, able to move around on crutches, but wearing a strong knee brace support, leg not allowed to touch ground. Two one-hour sessions per day of leg extension and flexion exercises from a prone position using 0.5 kg weight.
Stage 3	Twice-daily weight training continues; can now exert very light pressure with left foot on the ground.
Stage 4	Flexion now about 90 degrees, weight training load increased to 1.0 kg, also able to exert slightly more left leg pressure on the ground.
Stage 5	Now using one crutch, extension and flexion exercises more difficult as weight training load increased to 1.5 kg. Again, increased weight on left leg.
Stage 6	Two 15 min bicycle ergometer cycling sessions per day following each 1.5 hr weight training session. By the end, walking without crutches or help, but not quite as normal.

Yoko completed a Japanese version of the TESI on a daily basis during her rehabilitation, usually between 8.30 p.m. and 9.00 p.m. (with the exception of the three days immediately post-operation while she was still feeling the effects of the anaesthetic. These TESIs were completed on the fourth day). She also completed the TESI for five days before she entered hospital (to act as a baseline measure for comparative purposes). Thus, complete data for a total of sixty-five days were available. Her instructions were to mark the TESI items in accordance with her feelings over that particular day.

Space here does not allow all the TESI dimensions to be described and therefore the focus will be on overall pleasant and unpleasant emotions and bodily tension and effort stress. Figure 3.4 shows Yoko's self-reports of her overall pleasant and unpleasant emotions during the fifty-four-day rehabilitation period. As can be seen from Figure 3.4, her overall score for pleasant emotions was fairly consistent during the baseline period, in contrast to her score for overall unpleasant emotions, which showed more variation in the range of scores during this period.

The baseline mean score for overall pleasant emotions was 32 and that for overall unpleasant emotions was 25. Pleasant emotions appear to have decreased post-operation and never increased above the baseline mean during rehabilitation. A similar pattern for unpleasant emotions is also apparent, although there were two sharp increases – at the end of stage 2 and the beginning of stage 3, where scores doubled. These may have occurred as a result of the particular demands of the rehabilitation programme at those particular times. The decrease in pleasant emotions might have been expected, but the decrease in unpleasant emotions was not. Heil (1993), in his stage theory of response to injury, has suggested that an increase in unpleasant emotions might be expected as a consequence of athletes becoming injured. Clearly that was not the case with Yoko. Examining Yoko's scores on bodily stress and effort gives some indication of why this might have occurred.

Figure 3.5 shows a sharp increase in bodily stress scores occurring immediately post-operation and continuing throughout a gruelling fifty-four days of rehabilitation. This is not surprising in the circumstances. What is of interest here is that her scores for effort stress equal or exceed her scores for tension stress throughout the period. At no time, therefore, was there a mismatch between the stress she was experiencing from her body and her effort stress. This suggests that Yoko was successful in her attempts to cope with the after-effects of the operation and the demands of rehabilitation.

Note that the TESI can be used in a similar way in other sport contexts, such as monitoring emotions and stress of individual athletes or teams during travel to an overseas sport venue, during a series of games in a tournament, or even over a full season of matches. Psychological monitoring may allow sport psychologists to pinpoint problems associated with these examples and, where necessary, take action in the future to ensure that the problems do not recur.

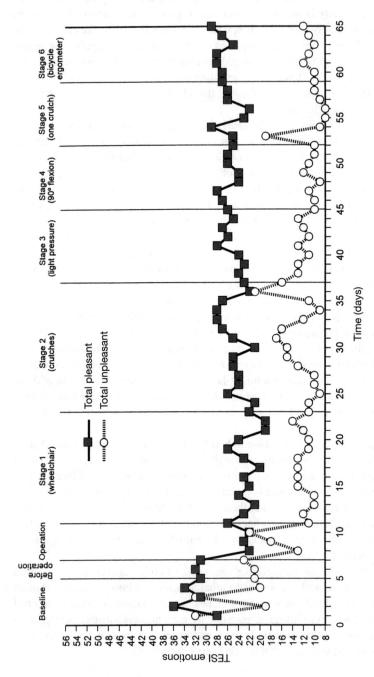

Figure 3.4 An elite athlete's overall TESI pleasant and unpleasant emotions during injury rehabilitation.

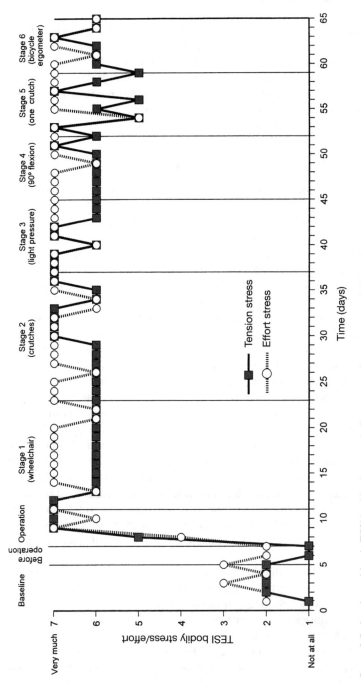

Figure 3.5 An elite athlete's TESI bodily stress and effort stress during injury rehabilitation.

MEASURING DOMINANCE

The first attempts at measuring metamotivational dominance involved the Telic Dominance Scale (TDS; Murgatroyd *et al.*, 1978) and, some time later, the Negativism Dominance Scale (NDS; McDermott and Apter, 1988). The Paratelic Dominance Scale (PDS; Cook and Gerkovich, 1993), which was developed especially for use with US populations, has to date not been used widely in sport research. The most recent and most comprehensive dominance measure is the Motivational Style Profile (MSP; Apter *et al.*, 1998).

The Telic and Negativism Dominance Scales

The TDS is a forty-two-item personality scale designed for use with adult subjects. It consists of three fourteen-item subscales which relate to different aspects of telic or paratelic dominance. The three subscales are known as *seriousmindedness* (SM), *planning orientation* (PO) and *arousal avoidance* (AA). These subscales measure how frequently a person is in a state of mind oriented to what he or she sees as: SM – serious ends, rather than playful activities; PO – activities which require planning ahead and a future orientation, rather than activities which are more unplanned and spontaneous; AA – arousal avoiding, rather than arousal seeking. The seriousmindedness subscale is taken as the defining subscale. Each subscale is scored independently, providing three subscale scores which can also be summed to provide an overall score for telic or paratelic dominance (that is, high scores indicate telic dominance, low scores indicate paratelic dominance).

The NDS is an eighteen-item personality scale designed for use with adolescent and adult subjects. It consists of two seven-item subscales (and four 'filler' items) which measure negativism or conformity dominance. The two subscales are known as *proactive negativism* (PN) and *reactive negativism* (RN). These subscales measure how frequently a person is in a state of mind oriented to what he or she sees as: PN – negativistic or rebellious behaviour for gratuitously provoking situations which are exciting and fun, or RN – reacting to frustration with feelings of resentment, and/or with vindictive or vengeful behaviour. As in the TDS, each subscale is scored independently, providing two subscale scores which can also be summed to provide an overall score for negativism or conformity dominance (that is, high scores indicate negativism dominance, low scores indicate conformity dominance).

The results of studies using the TDS and NDS have been well documented elsewhere (Kerr, 1997, 1999). Briefly, the TDS has shown that telic dominance is important in preference for and participation in different kinds of sports. For example, athletes from sports involving explosive action were found to be less telic dominant than athletes from endurance sports (Svebak and Kerr, 1989). Athletes who take part in risky or dangerous sports are less telic dominant than athletes from safe sports where there is little chance of personal injury or death (Chirivella and Martinez, 1994; Kerr, 1991; Kerr and Svebak, 1989; Summers and Stewart, 1993).

While telic dominance has been found to be important in preference for and participation in different kinds of sport, there is little evidence of differences between athletes performing at different levels within any single sport (e.g. Kerr and Cox, 1988; Cox and Kerr, 1989) or playing the same sport across different cultures (Kerr, 1988). However, when sample groups of athletes from several different sports are used, professional athletes have been found to be more telic dominant than amateur or recreational athletes (Kerr, 1987), as have masters athletes who continue to compete within their various age groups (Kerr and van Lienden, 1987).

For illustration purposes, Figure 3.6 shows a graphical comparison of the TDS subscale scores of high-level Dutch hockey players, hockey umpires and a control group of non-sports individuals who completed a Dutch version of the TDS. The hockey players and the control group were found to be significantly less serious-minded than the umpires. In addition, the hockey players scored significantly lower on arousal avoidance than the umpires and the control group, who had equal scores on the AA subscale. No important differences were found on the PO subscale scores, but significant differences between groups were found on total telic dominance scores.

Negativism dominance in athletes has also been explored. For example, professional soccer players were found to be more negativism dominant (in terms of reactive negativism) than long-distance runners (Vlaswinkel and Kerr, 1990).

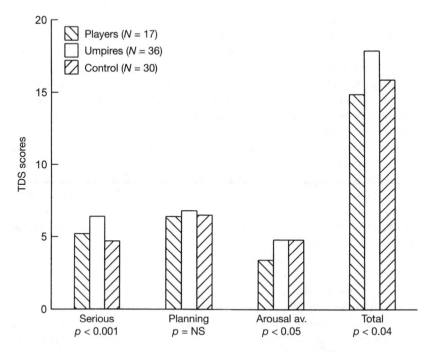

Figure 3.6 TDS subscale characteristics of field hockey players, umpires and a control group of non-sports practitioners.

Skilled teenage explosive-sport performers were found to be more negativism dominant (in terms of proactive negativism) than athletes from both endurance and team sports (Braathen and Svebak, 1992; Torild Hellandsig, 1998); and talented 18- and 19-year-old athletes who discontinued competition were found to be more negativism dominant (in terms of reactive negativism) than those who continued (Torild Hellandsig, 1998). Also, negativism-dominant losers in a squash competition experienced more unpleasantness after losing than losers who were less negativism dominant (Wilson and Phillips, 1995), and injuries incurred in sport have been shown to be related to proactive negativism (Cogan and Brown, 1998).

The Motivational Style Profile

The recently developed MSP is a seventy-item personality scale designed for use with adults. It consists of fourteen subscales which measure all forms of dominance associated with the four pairs of metamotivational states and some additional variables, as well as the salience of each type of dominance. Four subscales concern the *telic–paratelic*, *negativism–conformity* dimensions described above and two concern the *arousal avoidance–arousal seeking* dimension mentioned in connection with the TDS. Four other subscales consist of combinations of the *autic–alloic* and *mastery–sympathy* transactional metamotivational states. These have been labelled the *autic mastery–autic sympathy* and *alloic mastery–alloic sympathy* subscales. These subscales measure autic mastery – personal power and the need to dominate people, objects, situations or events; autic sympathy – personal affection and the need to be attractive to or sympathised with by others; alloic mastery – vicarious power and the need to enjoy the power of others through identifying with them; and alloic sympathy – vicarious affection and the need to experience pleasure by nurturing, sympathising with and giving to others. The four remaining subscales measure *optimism–pessimism*, *arousability* and *effortfulness*. Optimism and pessimism are self-explanatory. Arousability and effortfulness are aspects of response intensity concerned with the tendency to be easily aroused, and the energetic pursuit of goals, respectively. Rather than giving a total MSP score, the fourteen subscales are considered individually and used to produce a subscale profile and a salience profile (i.e., the relative importance of states) derived from the first ten subscales.

The MSP has been used in sport to investigate links between metamotivational dominance and eating disorders in athletes (Blaydon *et al.*, forthcoming). The results of this latter study will be discussed in Chapter 7, and readers are directed there for an illustration of how the MSP can be used in the sport context. Some preliminary work has also been carried out using a sport-specific version of the MSP which has been labelled the Motivational Style Profile for Sport and Exercise (MSPSE). In this version, minor changes to the MSP's general instructions were made to focus the respondent on their motivational experience in sport and exercise activities. The MSPSE has been used, for example, to examine the motivation of recreational sport participants (Au *et al.*, 2000).

CLOSING COMMENTS

This chapter has described a number of psychological measures which are available for use with athletes. They can be used by sport psychologists to assess athletes' operative metamotivational states, actual and preferred arousal levels, emotions and stress, and their metamotivational dominance. Although there are standard versions of these reversal theory measures, the instructions accompanying them can be adapted to suit the particular situation in which they are being used. The SOMIFA, for example, has generally been used post-performance, but it could easily be adapted for use before competition, or, in sports where there are natural breaks, during performances. Track-and-field athletics, where there are breaks between jumps, or racquet games where there are breaks between sets, are examples of sports which might allow testing as performance is ongoing. Further information about the measures described in this chapter and many examples of their use in the sport context are given by Kerr (1997, 1999).

Measuring instruments such as the SOMIFA can be extremely useful for sport psychologist and athlete. If, over time, however, an athlete becomes knowledgeable about reversal theory and familiar with the concepts of metamotivational states and reversals, it is possible that using questionnaire measures to identify operative states and arousal levels may become largely unnecessary. If used judiciously by the sport psychologist, the questionnaire becomes more of an educational tool than a mere measuring instrument and aids the athlete in becoming skilled at recognising his or her own operative metamotivational states and arousal levels. Paper-and-pencil monitoring becomes almost redundant. A good example of this can be found at the beginning of the next chapter.

SUGGESTED FURTHER READING

Kerr, J. H. (1997) 'We are the champions: winning and losing in sport', in J. H. Kerr, *Motivation and Emotion in Sport: Reversal Theory*, Hove: Psychology Press.
Kerr, J. H. (1997) 'Into sport: aspects of participation and preference', in J. H. Kerr, *Motivation and Emotion in Sport: Reversal Theory*, Hove: Psychology Press.
Apter, M. J. (1999) 'Measurement challenges in reversal theory sport research', in J. H. Kerr (ed.) *Experiencing Sport: Reversal Theory*, Chichester: Wiley.

FOR DISCUSSION

Figures 3.7A and 3.7B show two SOMIFA section As completed by Chris and Mary, two elite performers competing in the World Triathlon Championships. Compare their responses and consider:

1   What is the operative metamotivational state combination for each athlete?

Name: Chris   Age: 25
Date: Sport: Triathlon
Occasion/Event: World Triathlon Championships   Outcome: 3rd overall

INSTRUCTIONS:
Please answer the following questions about the sporting event or the specific part of the event indicated.

I Choose one from each of the following pairs of statements which most closely describes your feelings during the performance. (Check the appropriate box in each case.) Please try to judge in terms of **THE TIME YOU WERE ACTUALLY PERFORMING** (NOT how you felt immediately before or after, how you should have felt, how you feel now, or how you usually would have felt).

I WANTED TO:

1.a ☑ achieve something important to me (e.g., status, money, improved skill).
1.b ☐ simply enjoy the fun of participating in the event.

2.a ☐ keep to the instructions and expectations of coaches and others.
2.b ☑ do my own thing whatever the consequences.

3.a ☑ be tough with and dominating over my opponent(s) during performance.
3.b ☐ be friendly and sympathetic with my opponent(s) during performance.

4.a ☑ perform well for myself
4.b ☐ perform well for others (e.g. my coach, team, supporters, etc.)

5. Of all the items which you chose above, which is the **ONE**
    that you were most aware of during performance.   ┌──────┐
    (Please write the number and letter in this box.)   │ 1a │
                                                                       └──────┘

Figure 3.7A A copy of the SOMIFA (section A only) completed by Chris, a competitor in the World Triathlon Championships.

Name: Mary   Age: 31
Date: Sport: Triathlon
Occasion/Event: World Triathlon Championships   Outcome: top 20 in age group

INSTRUCTIONS:
Please answer the following questions about the sporting event or the specific part of the event indicated.

I Choose one from each of the following pairs of statements which most closely describes your feelings during the performance. (Check the appropriate box in each case.) Please try to judge in terms of **THE TIME YOU WERE ACTUALLY PERFORMING** (NOT how you felt immediately before or after, how you should have felt, how you feel now, or how you usually would have felt).

I WANTED TO:

1.a ☐ achieve something important to me (e.g., status, money, improved skill).
1.b ☑ simply enjoy the fun of participating in the event.

2.a ☐ keep to the instructions and expectations of coaches and others.
2.b ☑ do my own thing whatever the consequences.

3.a ☐ be tough with and dominating over my opponent(s) during performance.
3.b ☑ be friendly and sympathetic with my opponent(s) during performance.

4.a ☑ perform well for myself
4.b ☐ perform well for others (e.g. my coach, team, supporters, etc.)

5. Of all the items which you chose above, which is the **ONE**
    that you were most aware of during performance.   ┌──────┐
    (Please write the number and letter in this box.)   │ 1b │
                                                                       └──────┘

Figure 3.7B A copy of the SOMIFA (section A only) completed by Mary, a competitor in the World Triathlon Championships.

2   What are the similarities and the differences between the two athletes' state combinations and what do their responses indicate about their metamotivational states during the triathlon event?

3   Which state is salient for each athlete and what does this suggest about each athlete's motivation for competing on this occasion?

After you have considered and discussed these questions, see the following section for more information about Chris and Mary.

4   Research by Svebak and Kerr (1989) found that, given a free choice, paratelic-dominant Australian students preferred and took part in sports such as baseball, cricket, surfing and windsurfing, and telic-dominant students preferred and took part in sports such as long-distance running and rowing. How can this result be explained?

FURTHER INFORMATION ON CHRIS AND MARY

Chris

Chris is a 25-year-old semi-professional who spends his summers racing in Europe. He is from a running background and runs for more than twenty hours per week. Although he has a degree and works through the winter months, his life revolves around racing. He does not want to do anything but race and train. During the previous summer, he did eighteen races in sixteen weeks – he said he never felt so tired in his life, but plans to go back again next year. In these World Triathlon Championships, he finished in third place.

Mary

Mary is 31 and used to swim competitively for a national regional team, but did not really take it seriously. Later she took up swimming with a triathlon squad to keep fit, and eventually started doing a few local triathlon events. In 1996, after successfully competing in a qualification event, she decided to do the Hawaii Ironman event and has been racing long-distance and Ironman events ever since. Her best time is 10.40 hours. She works part-time and completes fourteen to twenty hours of training a week, and plans to do at least three or four Ironman events during the current year. She has been described as always laughing and a real rebel. She reputedly never watches her diet, enjoys drinking and is always the last to leave the post-race party. In these World Triathlon Championships, she finished in the top twenty within her age group.

Chapter 4

Identifying performance motivation problems

INTRODUCTION

This chapter takes a closer look at how reversal theory can be applied to detecting and solving performance motivation problems in athletes. The basis for this approach to counselling athletes can be found in the reversal theory-based clinical work of Murgatroyd and Apter (1984, 1986), who highlighted a number of *reversal process problems*, including the problem at focus here, that of *inappropriate reversals* (Lafreniere *et al.*, 2001; Murgatroyd, 1987c; Murgatroyd and Apter, 1984, 1986) The reversal theory approach to counselling and psychotherapy was first applied to psychological interventions with athletes by Kerr (1993).

The central focus of this chapter is a detailed examination of an elite female triathlete's experience while competing in her first World Triathlon Championship. This case shows the dynamic nature of the reversal process and provides a rich description of how the process operates during the preparation stages and actual performance at a competitive sport event. The triathlete's experience will then be examined with reference to Murgatroyd and Apter's work in psychotherapy. In addition, the reversal theory concept of paratelic protective frames will be explored and related to the notion of facilitative–debilitative anxiety from the sport psychology literature.

JACKIE: TRIATHLETE AT THE WORLD CHAMPIONSHIPS

Background

Jackie, currently a university student, was a former top-level junior swimmer. She was first asked to do a triathlon for fun in 1996 and actually performed well. It was about a year later, after she had bought a bike, that she tried it again. Her first year of competing was 1998 and, considering it was her first, it turned out to be a very successful year. Ranked fourth in her country and eighth in Asia, Jackie made her national squad in February 1998. Her goal was to be ranked in the top fifty to sixty in the world by the end of 1999. Jackie had acquired enough knowledge of reversal theory to allow her to self-analyse and recognise her own metamotivation and feelings when training and performing, and these she 'wrote up' as daily entries in a competition diary she kept at a recent Triathlon World Championship. The diary entries are preceded by Jackie's comments about training, which provide some clues about her general motivation as a triathlete:

> I find the training very therapeutic and it channels my mind, but I wouldn't do it if I didn't compete. I have now become very good at listening to my body – I tend to take big breaks. I never race back to back and if I don't want to train, I don't. I get really annoyed if I am pushed to train when I don't want to by my obsessive training partner so, although I tend to be of a telic nature when it comes to training, this tends to be more so when I have a competition to train for. If I don't have a goal or competition, I tend to cut down and use it as a release from study. I feel I have a healthy balance. I could, however, I think, get the bug if I felt it would take me places.

World Triathlon diary

Day 1

1st day in Bienne, joined the rest of the Squad. At the moment feeling very relaxed and looking forward to getting on with some serious training. Staying in the Elite Centre for Sport and Exercise Research and Teacher Training. The facilities are excellent. There are many elite athletes around, most from the States competing in track and field on the European leg of the Golden Grand Prix. Being surrounded by these people is very encouraging and inspirational.

The morning session started at 7 am with an easy 1.5 hour spin on the bike. I feel very telic and conformist. Most of my training is done by myself at home and I never have a coach telling me what to do. It actually feels nice to be told what to do and when to do it. Of course I am doing everything I am told.

Whilst on the training ride, I found that I had become very autic–mastery. I have travelled with my cycle buddy, who is completely telic nuts, since deciding to go to the Worlds. Today she was lagging behind; I would normally wait, but I wanted to stay with the rest of the team to see how I was doing in terms of my strength and capabilities. After, I felt very guilty because I think, had it been the other way round, she would have waited and she did seem a little upset because she felt that if she couldn't keep up then she shouldn't be here. I became very sympathetic after the session as I tried to console her and make her feel better. I spent the next swimming session coaching her and giving her tips and encouragement (alloic–sympathy). The swim again was easy and I stayed in extra time to complete the session after everyone had left.

While running this evening before dinner, I began to feel tired. I wanted to cut the run short and walk back and definitely not do any hills, but by this time my partner had reversed to telic-mastery after feeling worthless. She was now really strong and determined. Now feeling very anxious as I am confused about what to do; I would normally listen to my body but, being a little bit competitive and conformist as we have been told to run for a certain amount of time, I decide to run with her, even play a little bit once I got in the swing of things by running slightly ahead. It has annoyed me that she has decided to go against the scheduled training session and asked me to run with her and she is running really hard, I think she is a little annoyed with me for leaving her behind. Again I have reversed from being sympathetic to mastery, quite selfish actually. I felt very relieved when the run was over. The warm down was very interesting – my training partner completely reversed and the anxiety was very low; it actually turned into a pleasant run as we joked and laughed about our competitiveness. At one point I turned my ankle on a rock and she stopped to check I was alright – I wonder if that would have happened a few minutes before. I find the whole competitive thing really silly, and it really raises my anxiety level to really uncomfortable levels, especially since outside competition and on easy sessions, she is my friend. I have certainly become more telic as I strive to achieve my goals set, but I am not really enjoying any of it. I don't get it, I guess that is the nature of the game.

Day 2

No morning session due to rain. Was very relieved, feeling quite tired. Swim session later felt more positive, better than yesterday. Rescheduled bike in the afternoon was scary, I had never done anything like this before and it hurt. Three times 1.5 km hill climbs flat out speed with a transition to run 500 metres fast after each bike climb. The girls started first, the competitiveness was strong between us, it was quite nasty. We are such good friends, too. I was tired and lagged behind on the bike. I remained telic, focused, but reversed briefly while I tried to talk myself into pulling out but reversed right back to telic and drove up the hill with what energy I had left. I became more determined that I was going to beat or at least scare them on the next rounds which I managed, thank god (autic–mastery); still not feeling confident and my anxiety levels are very high which I can't seem to control. I don't think it is helping me physically but definitely making me more determined, especially over my fellow female team members. I don't feel this way with the male squad members, I seem to feel more of a team with them; I do most of my swimming training with them as it is my strongest event and I definitely enjoy my sessions more and seem to do much better. I feel more alloic–mastery in this situation. They don't seem to freak out and are so much calmer, more laid back, but determined and motivated, which I seemed to feed from. I feel that I am becoming more mastery and telic with little reversal to the paratelic state even when training is over – my anxiety is too high and things don't feel good and are not going to plan. I seem to tolerate the anxiety and even feed from it but I am more aware of it than usual and it is making me tired and uncomfortable.

Day 3

Morning run, felt quite good, felt my first reversal to the negativistic state when I decided not to follow the group in sprinting up a hill. My goal was to have a recovery run and that certainly wasn't. I was ridiculed for not following but I had my reasons and was sticking to them. I could feel the competitiveness from my partner as she felt mastery over me because she made it up the hill. It only made me even more determined to do well on the next session. The competitiveness was actually becoming amusing although only the men were laughing. I did feel very intimidated and almost not worthy of such an event as the World Champs. I have done many world class events at swimming but never felt so incapable – I really put it down to lack of experience. This inexperience is making my anxiety levels too high. I don't know what to expect, or if I am achieving my goals at the appropriate level that I should be.

Day 4

Worst day yet. I just don't understand why nothing is going as planned. Training was brilliant before I left and now I just can't seem to get it together. We went for a long bike ride, and after three hours – the coach was away at the time, but before leaving said not to climb the 7 km hill home so near to the race – a call was made on the way back to climb the hill. I didn't feel like it, but felt silly for not wanting to so just conformed and followed. Big mistake! I fell so far back, even in past sessions I could keep up with these men and, as for the rest of the girls being so far in front, something was wrong, but I didn't feel tired, just had nothing there and I was having real problems dealing with it. The rest of the ride had been good and all of a sudden I wasn't doing too well. Several times during the ride I could feel myself reverse and want to just stop and I would reverse again and drive myself up the hill – my speed would significantly change as I reversed into the telic state. As the ride progressed, I became less mastery-oriented and started to concentrate on the goal of the ride instead of being concerned about my peers. Although being upset for not being able to compete with them, I had achieved my new set goal and so ended up fairly happy. It was at this point that the rest of the trip improved as I started to focus on me and what I wanted to achieve rather than what every one else was trying to do and trying to do better. It was interesting also how I had to reset my goals in order to continue in the telic state on this ride and also how long it look me to make these decisions. In a race it would have been much harder to deal with. I think had it been a race I would have probably dropped out, I wonder if things could turn around fast enough to pull a race back together. My goals for the Worlds had been set from this point. I wanted to do a good time – I felt that I deserved it – but more importantly, I had to beat my training partner. Her mastery and confidence had annoyed me and I knew I was capable of doing it.

Day 5

Day off today. My change in attitude is significant – I had really calmed down; my anxiety has reduced significantly and I feel less uneasy with my peers and more focused and in control. I am certainly in the paratelic state, I want to have fun, and I don't feel so trapped in a telic state where I worry about achieving my goals. In the paratelic state, my anxiety levels seem more controllable, or I am just able to redirect my anxiety where it doesn't affect my performance. My goals are written down, I now just want to race. I had a talk with one of the US track athletes at his training session. I found him again really encouraging and he motivated me to want to do well through his drive and determination to want to achieve great things. By the end of the day, I was much more sympathetic toward my training buddy and I sat and explained the purpose of my diary and what I had written and we laughed and joked about it and she agreed with many of the feelings I had expressed. It seemed to clear the air as we talked about what we wanted to achieve, and we both reversed to a sympathy state as we continued to talk and express admiration for each other.

Day 6

All of a sudden it clicked today. I felt strong and very telic during my sessions and managed to reverse easily back to the paratelic state as we took it easy in the evening, my anxiety was low and I felt strong. I was way in front of my peers today and kept up with the men easily. At last. I reversed into the alloic state as my training friend seemed to be suffering from the dreaded bike legs that I had a few days previous; I turned around and pulled her up the hill. When thinking back, I definitely also reversed to a sympathy state in order to do this. It made me feel good to help my friend and I was reassured that training had gone so well.

Day 7

I feel tired and as a consequence my anxiety is high, although my training is feeling good and I seem to be just dealing with it, although I would say that it doesn't make me happy and I seem to be eating, drinking and sleeping triathlons. I had a dream that I couldn't get my foot in my bike shoe after the swim and the word is that there is a really bad hill in the race. In my dream, I had to try a struggle the whole 40 km with my foot on top of my shoe, Now

I'm stressed, although everyone laughed at me when I told them. I just feel that I am going into the unknown. It is not like swimming 100 meters in a race where your tactics are hard and fast and if you're strong you will do well. In triathlon, situations change from race to race – there is always 'what ifs'. You can have a plan, but it is knowing how to deal with them if they happen. Going into a race with too much expectation can be devastating, as something uncontrollable may happen and you have to have a game plan to back it up. It can be psychologically tough.

Day 8

I am so ready to race, I have my goals and now a different attitude. I have reversed into the paratelic state and am much less tense and convinced myself to enjoy the event. I have never done a course like this and I have never raced people of this standard before. It is pretty frightening with many scary people with scary looking legs walking around. I am now very excited and pretty composed, as I soak up the atmosphere of the event. We have done the bike course and the 'hill' is a lump compared to back home, so my anxiety levels are much lower and I have a general focus on the race. I really have to beat my training buddy – she is far too confident that she is going to beat me on the bike leg!!! I love the competition side now as I have grown more confident in my own abilities and I just want to race. All the stress of the last week has passed and I'm ready.

Day 9

Up early for the race – slept quite well, went through my normal race routine last night and now feel excited and composed. Met one of the New Zealand champions who raced yesterday, who gave us some pre-race tips. As he described the race course as he biked it, I could feel myself reverse into the telic state as I imagined the course and set my goals accordingly and imagined how I would feel as I competed, telic–mastery, and conformist as I listened and decided to do as the athlete had suggested. This calmed me down a lot and I felt mastery. I want to put all my efforts into this race.

Before the race felt good – although anxious, it felt good and I was quite composed – or confident would be a better word, I felt ready. It was cold and I deliberated whether to put a sweater on during the bike leg, would this waste time? I would decide after the swim. Everyone's worries were stressing me out so I took myself off to calm down, and took a long walk to the start. The swim I always find frustrating as I am a swimmer and quite strong, however, I never seem to do the swim leg justice. Although, comparatively speaking, I did well, I still have to work on this bit. I found that my mind doesn't pull together on this leg because you are worried about where you are going. This race was no exception. I couldn't put my head down and I found I got angry, and became a bit negative at certain stages, having to pull myself out of this state to remain competitive and focused. The bike transition was fine and I managed to get my foot into the shoe!!!! I took the first lap easy to see how it was and recover from the swim. Advice from the guys yesterday said that it would get really hard after three legs. It did, but everything went really well and I remained composed and competitive. The hills were easy and I was not fazed by any of them. As I came off the bike in the transition, I started to feel cold and I couldn't feel my legs. So I put my hat on, took some energy GU [a glucose and caffeine energy supplement] and put my head down and decided to just run until I could start pushing it. This normally happens after 2 km. After a while, not really remembering the last 7 mins or so, must have been a bit delirious, I realised that I had taken the wrong fork of the run and was heading toward the finish line and I had only just started. I REVERSED!!!! Freaked out!!! I nearly pulled out, how embarrassing, what would every one say. What do I do, pull out, turn around and run back? That would be embarrassing, I wasn't sure how the run course went, so I couldn't decide what to do. My head was all over the place and in the end decided to keep going and do a bit more on the run and see what happens. I have lost any chance of staying in the top 10 and I may even get disqualified but I didn't want to stop, I felt so good and strong. Once I had made a decision (in the telic state) to finish I then completely reversed to the paratelic and negativistic states, I wasn't going to pull out even if I had run the wrong way but there was no point pushing it so I slowed down. I was angry and confused as I wasn't sure what to do, or if I was doing the right thing. I had to laugh, or I may have cried. I enjoyed every minute of it and you can bet that I will be there next year because I know I could do well. I still beat my training buddy. I was pleased about that but it was close – she still wants my place on the team.

As it turned out, Jackie was not disqualified and finished in twenty-ninth place. She was pleased with her place, but felt she could have achieved a better time.

Postscript to the World Championship

It is interesting that just two weeks after the World Championship, while she was still recovering, Jackie was 'forced' by officials to take part in a selection race. Although she was still enthusiastic about competing in triathlons for fun, this made her angry. A week before the race, she went for a few rides and runs and, to her surprise, she felt fantastic. After this, she decided to comply with what the officials wanted and try to improve on her performance in the World Championships, becoming, in her own words, 'telic–conformist–mastery oriented'. However, on the race day she was tired, yawning all the time (also a somatic symptom of anxiety) and she was not at all composed, feeling that she could not control her high anxiety. All this contributed to a very negative frame of mind ('my paratelic and negativistic states were back'), and she just did not want to race. Her swim was very poor, and halfway around the bike course, having no energy in her legs, she pulled out. At this point she was very angry and really did not want to be there, so she stopped. She also felt rebellious, comparing herself to Denis Rodman, the controversial US basketball player. Jackie had never pulled out of a triathlon before, and certainly not in a selection race. In hindsight, she felt that she should not have competed in this race ('the reversal to paratelic state after being so telic at the Worlds was strong – I had no real goal and the race wasn't important to me').

Insights from Jackie's diary entries

As her diary entries illustrate, Jackie was reasonably proficient at recognising her operative metamotivational state(s), when reversals occurred, and the associated emotions that she experienced. Some of these reversals were undesired and stressful for Jackie and appeared to, for example, have interfered with her final preparation for the championships. At least some of these undesired reversals can be put down to her lack of competition experience, but they are also examples of a recognised reversal process problem known as inappropriate reversals (Lafreniere *et al.*, 2001; Murgatroyd, 1987c; Murgatroyd and Apter, 1984, 1986; and see Chapter 5). In addition, the frequency with which she refers to high-arousal emotions such as anxiety, excitement and anger sometimes occurring very close together suggests possible frequent and very rapid reversals between telic and paratelic and negativistic and conformist states.

An athlete performing at this level must learn to cope with a number of stressors, any one of which can act as a trigger for reversal (Kerr, 1993). Some performance-related stressors include receiving unpleasant input from observers, coaches, teammates or opponents; making an error during performance; reacting to the success or failure of an opponent (or colleague); contending with the poor judgement of an official; an unfavourable game score; and dealing with the pain of an injury (Anshel, 1990). In addition, athletes may have to cope with other types of stressors related to time management, finances and the media, as well as in personal relationships with others (e.g. Crocker and Graham, 1995; Gould *et al.*, 1993; Madden *et al.*, 1990).

Jackie's entries suggest that she was subject to at least some of these performance-related stressors. During the early part of her final preparation in the days prior to the race, for example, she frequently experienced high arousal as unpleasant anxiety (telic–conformity) or anger (telic– negativism). This was caused by Jackie being 'forced' to do extra training when she felt tired and lacked energy (even on one occasion going against her coach's advice and trying the 7 kilometre hill climb). In spite of her inexperience in competing in the triathlon, however, Jackie was also sensitive to these stressors and, with regard to her interaction with teammates, sensitive to which transactional states were operative, and she was able to recognise when reversals in transactional states took place. This is illustrated by a number of her comments about her relationship with male competitors and other members of her national squad, especially her training partner, with whom she had an uncomfortable relationship during the early days of preparation.

By day 5, Jackie had resolved her differences with her training partner and changed her approach by focusing on her own performance and not what others were doing. On the following day her training 'clicked', although on the day after she was feeling 'stressed' and worrying about things that could go wrong during the race. This was probably as a result of being back in the telic state under conditions of high arousal, and it is likely that another inappropriate reversal had occurred. On the day before the race, the stress had gone and she was 'ready to race'. Here she was full of the confidence about performance that can be attributed to an autic–mastery state combination. The mastery state may well have been salient at this time. She was still experiencing reversals (especially between telic and paratelic states), but seemed more comfortable with them.

There were two especially noteworthy occurrences on the day of the race. The first concerns Jackie's state of mind just prior to the race. At the competition site pre-race, she found that other athletes' worries about the forthcoming race were infectious and she herself began to feel stressed as a result. She moved away from the other athletes in order to reduce her arousal level (calm down) and took a long walk to the start. It seems likely that she was in the telic state at this point and this increased arousal was experienced as unpleasant tension stress. However, she recognised this and adopted her own arousal modulation technique to remedy the situation (see Figure 4.1). As pointed out previously, an athlete experiencing unpleasant high arousal has two choices for intervention. He or she can either try to induce a reversal, in this case to the paratelic state, or attempt to decrease felt arousal. In this instance, Jackie was able to benefit from several days of monitoring her own feelings. By recognising that she was being affected by the other athletes and 'taking avoiding action', Jackie chose the latter option and was able to decrease her arousal to her preferred level and remain in the same metamotivational (telic) state.

The second concerns the reversal (or several reversals) which occurred during the running section of the triathlon as a result of Jackie making a judgement error while 'a bit delirious', mistaking the route and heading off in the wrong direction.

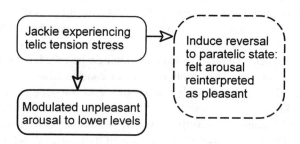

Figure 4.1 The intervention options and strategy of choice used by Jackie to alleviate pre-competitive anxiety.

This mistake induced a contingent reversal. When she realised what had happened, she decided to continue the race (a goal-oriented decision made while Jackie was in the telic state). Once the decision to continue was made, she said that she reversed back to the paratelic state in combination with the negativistic state. At this point she said that she was 'feeling angry and confused', and later that she 'enjoyed every minute of it'. However, according to reversal theory, anger is an unpleasant emotion which arises from telic–negativism. It is possible that Jackie was experiencing a series of frequent and rapid reversals at this point which might explain the apparently contradictory feelings that she reported. Another possibility is that the anger Jackie was feeling at this point was parapathic anger (see Chapter 1). If so, her anger would have been experienced in a paratelic frame as pleasant, thus contributing to her overall hedonic tone and general feelings of enjoyment, in spite of her mistake.

PARAPATHIC EMOTIONS

As pointed out in Chapter 1, and above, paratelic protective frames allow emotions, like Jackie's experience of anger, which are usually experienced as unpleasant to be experienced as pleasant. They also have an important part to play in gaining an understanding of athletes' experience of anxiety, another unpleasant emotion sometimes reported by athletes. Paratelic frames of experience are thought to be based on a perception of confidence, or a sense of distance from real physical or emotional harm, especially in risk sports and other dangerous activities (Apter, 1992; Kerr, 1997). In many sports, the social risk that athletes face – for example, the threat to their self-esteem – may be just as threatening as the risk of physical harm should they not perform at their best. Paratelic frames may also occur, therefore, during competitive sport. Elite canoe slalom research results (Males and Kerr, 1996; Males *et al.*, 1998) indicated that, while some of the canoeists did experience unpleasant anxiety and stress and coped by using breathing and visualisation techniques,

> [t]he overall motivation for participation was often paratelic – the paddler simply enjoyed racing. This then reversed to telic seriousness around specific events, which in turn allowed increased significance and therefore potentially greater goal satisfaction. The increased significance also increased felt arousal, which was then converted via the paratelic frame into excitement. Without the paratelic frame, participation in major events could be unpleasant because high felt arousal would be experienced as telic tension stress, and frightening because failure would represent a threat to self-esteem and personal meaning.
> (Males, 1999, pp. 122–123)

Males (1999) also explored some of the strategies that elite slalom canoeists adopted for creating and maintaining a paratelic confidence frame around competitive performance in order to change their experience of anxiety. These included:

1   Reducing the importance of the event: by putting it into perspective compared to the rest of the canoeist's life.
2   Self-talk: reinforcing process goals rather than outcome goals.
3   Distraction: talking with competitors or officials.
4   Concentration: on aspects of technique and 'in the moment' awareness rather than dwelling on the future results.
5   Listening to loud rock music: to maintain pleasant high arousal.

Sport psychology research has frequently attempted to uncover the relationship between athletes' self-reported anxiety and subsequent performance (e.g. Burton, 1988; Krane and Williams, 1987; Man et al., 1995; Raglin and Turner, 1993). However, the results have been far from conclusive (e.g. Klein, 1990). The inconclusive nature of the results may be due in part to a number of measurement issues concerning anxiety research in sport (e.g. Burton and Naylor 1997; Kerr, 1997). However, leaving aside criticisms about measurement, it also seems possible that a close examination of athletes' reports of experiencing anxiety would reveal that paratelic protective frames were in operation. Athletes frequently talk about anxiety in a way that has been labelled by some researchers as 'positive anxiety' which facilitates good performance (Jones and Swain, 1992, 1995; Swain and Jones, 1993). Indeed, it may be that 'real' anxiety is debilitative to performance and so-called 'facilitative anxiety' is in fact parapathic anxiety experienced through a paratelic protective frame as outlined in reversal theory.

CLOSING COMMENTS

Following Jackie through her self-reported experiences at the World Triathlon Championship, including some of her personal trials and tribulations as well as successes, served to provide further insight into the theoretical arguments of reversal theory. Through Jackie's own reversal theory analysis, it was possible to identify when inappropriate reversals and undesired changes in felt arousal and felt transactional outcome took place, and her description showed how easily they can occur during sports events. This may be especially true for athletes, like Jackie, who are short of experience in major championships.

It was also possible to identify Jackie's preferred or customary performance state combinations, especially during the days and hours immediately before the race. However, unexpected situational or environmental events are common during competition and these may induce inappropriate reversals and place athletes under stress at any time. Athletes who have the knowledge and ability to cope, by initiating some form of cognitive intervention strategy to deal with the types of stressors outlined earlier, are at an advantage.

It was also demonstrated how, for Jackie, a knowledge of reversal theory helped her to identify and understand her own motivation and emotions and, on occasion, modify her behaviour while at the World Triathlon Championships. In her own words,

> Thinking about metamotivational states and reversals during this time proved very interesting. It was quite helpful to have an understanding of what is going on. What surprised me the most was how often my mood, anxiety, composure and motivational states changed, when they occurred and how lack of experience affected all these. Having realised I had reversed, I found I could rationalise and deal with the situation and how I felt and then decide what I was going to do, even provoke a reversal back.
>
> I have a few more races left – one important one and one not so important. I will keep track, as I think it is helpful for me. Particularly during a race, such as a triathlon, so many reversals take place. I think it is the people that have fewer reversals that do better; staying in the telic–mastery state is tough, especially when things don't go well.

The concept of a paratelic protective frame being created by athletes is an especially important one. While it is relatively easy to understand how protective frames might work in dangerous or risk sport activities (Apter, 1992; Kerr, 1997), careful consideration reveals that they could be just as relevant in sports with a lesser risk of physical injury. Whether or not this concept may also be useful in clarifying the debate about facilitative–debilitative anxiety will require the attention of sport psychology researchers.

Chapter 5 will extend the application of reversal theory to counselling for performance motivation problems and, especially, inappropriate reversals in athletes. A number of cases in which athletes consulted a sport psychologist are examined and the cognitive intervention strategies which were subsequently used, following consultation, are presented.

SUGGESTED FURTHER READING

Males, J. R., Kerr, J. H. and Gerkovich, M. (1998) 'Metamotivational states during canoe slalom competition: a qualitative analysis using reversal theory', *Journal of Applied Sport Psychology* 10: 184–200.

Lafreniere, K. D., Ledgerwood, D. M. and Murgatroyd, S. (2001) 'Psychopathology, therapy and counselling', in M. J. Apter (ed.) *Motivational Styles in Everyday Life: A Guide to Reversal Theory*, Washington, DC: American Psychological Association.

Purcell, I. P. (1999) 'Verbal protocols and structured interviews for motives, plans and decisions in golf', in J. H. Kerr (ed.) *Experiencing Sport: Reversal Theory*, Chichester: Wiley.

FOR DISCUSSION

Ken: disappointed triple jumper

Ken, now 22 years old, started triple-jumping at junior high school, aged 14. At senior high school, his physical education teacher was an ex-elite-level athlete who competed in the track-and-field athletic events at the Los Angeles Olympics. Under the tutelage of his teacher, Ken became his country's national high school champion and, for several years now, he has been national champion at senior level. He recently travelled abroad to compete in the Asian Games. On his first attempt in the competition, he made a reasonable jump, 0.22 metre below his personal best. After his first jump, however, there was a stiff headwind blowing. As athletes are allowed one minute waiting time after they are called, Ken waited on the second, third and fourth jumps for the wind to drop. It did not drop. Unfortunately, by waiting as long as possible each time before jumping, he lost concentration and then, because of overstriding over the first part of the approach run, he made three no-jumps. On the fifth and sixth jumps he decided not to wait for a decrease in the wind, but just to go for it. Two more failures. He finished in fourth place, on the strength of his first jump. Ken was not at all satisfied with his performance. He felt that the wind had affected him mentally. He had thought about the wind too much and this had distracted him, resulting in a loss of concentration which affected his jumping ability and his final placing. He had expected to put in a much better performance and admitted that he always has a problem with concentration when he goes abroad to compete.

Analyse this short case from the reversal theory point of view.

1 What can be said about Ken's state of mind before his first jump?
2 What brought about the change after his first jump and how did this affect his state of mind?
3 How would you describe Ken's performance motivation problem?
4 Was Ken's decision to 'just go for it' on the last two jumps an appropriate way of handling the problem? What might have prompted this decision?

Counselling athletes with inappropriate reversal problems

INTRODUCTION

In competition, it is important that the performer (and sport psychologist) endeavour to ensure that the metamotivational states preferred for optimal performance are operative and accompanied by appropriate levels of influential performance variables, such as felt arousal, felt negativism and felt transactional outcome. In the previous chapter, a good example of arousal modulation at the competition site was shown by Jackie when other competitors' high levels of anxiety began to 'get to her' before the World Triathlon Championships. She used her own common sense and dealt with the problem in her own straightforward, uncomplicated way. On that occasion, her strategy seemed to work in a satisfactory fashion. As was pointed out in Chapter 1, for athletes experiencing too high or too low levels of felt arousal (or other metamotivational variables), cognitive interventions using recognised techniques such as progressive relaxation may be necessary (Kerr 1993, 1997). This requires that the athletes concerned should be trained in, and have practised, these techniques. However, having the knowledge and ability to induce reversals at the competition site when necessary may be just as important an aid to athletes as their ability to modulate felt arousal levels.

On the day of the competition and at the competition site, the experienced athlete is likely to utilise personal performance routines which have been developed through his or her previous experience. Athletes may become skilled at regulating metamotivational states (and metamotivational variables, such as felt arousal) conducive to optimal performance through their personal performance routines (Boutcher, 1990; Kerr, 1993). In other words, through their preparatory cognitive and somatic activities, athletes may be able to induce reversals and make their customary performance state or preferred performance metamotivational state combination operative. Reversal theory argues that athletes cannot consciously induce reversals, but that they can indirectly control their own reversals by deliberately bringing about a change in their environment, or in other ways (Apter, 1982, 1989; Kerr and Tacon, 1999). As Kerr (1993) pointed out, athletes' methods for inducing reversals may be very similar to those used by gamblers, smokers, drug addicts and others (Brown, 1991; Miller, 1985; O'Connell *et al.*, 1997) in their 'personal planning to optimize mood' (Thayer, 1989, p. 174).

A good example of an athlete's personal planning to induce customary performance states is given by Males (1999). An interview with the athlete, a slalom canoeist (C), indicated that he performed poorly on his first attempt at the slalom course and realised that he was in an inappropriate state of mind for performing optimally in his second trial. He took himself away from a place which was crowded with other boisterous athletes and retired to the quiet interior of his van. Here he took a short nap and then concentrated on getting himself into his familiar pre-performance relaxed state before focusing in on his performance. This relaxed state changed again to a familiar feeling of excitement about twenty minutes before his second, more successful, attempt at the slalom course. If we interpret his behaviour in reversal theory terms, we can say that the canoeist placed himself in an environment where he could both reduce felt arousal and induce the telic state, and then he later reversed to his usual pre-competitive paratelic state.

How can the sport psychologist help an athlete who has an ongoing performance motivation problem which can be diagnosed as being the result of inappropriate reversals? In the next section of the chapter, case material will be used to illustrate how a sport psychologist can use the reversal theory approach in solving inappropriate reversal problems. Before we move on to the cases, however, it should first be pointed out that the reversal theory approach to counselling athletes is an eclectic one. It provides a systematic theoretical foundation on which to base intervention work with athletes, and may utilise a range of counselling and therapeutic techniques, for example psychosynthesis (Assagioli, 1969, 1990), Rational Emotive Therapy (Ellis, 1962, 1970), humour as a counselling tool (Murgatroyd, 1987a), paradoxical intention and meditation (Murgatroyd, 1987b), or drama therapy and role-play techniques (Fontana and Valente, 1993). In this sense, reversal theory is rather like a computer operating system such as the Microsoft Windows system. Windows operates as a program manager on which other computer software programs can be integrated and run. If used correctly, the Windows program adds to the effectiveness and efficiency of the person using the computer, and so it is with reversal theory when applied to athlete counselling.

The following four short cases were contributed by Jonathan Males, whose London-based company, Performance1, counsels British athletes and other performers. The cases were first presented at the Seventh International Conference on Reversal Theory, held in Melbourne, Australia, in 1995 and the First International Workshop on Motivation and Emotion in Sport, held in Tsukuba, Japan, in 1996. They follow a format of first providing the relevant background history of the athlete, followed by the content of sessions, interventions used and their relationship to reversal theory, and, finally, the outcomes of the work. Only the elements of the sessions that are relevant to reversal theory are reported, therefore the cases are not complete records of all work carried out with the athletes.

COUNSELLING ATHLETES WITH INAPPROPRIATE REVERSAL PROBLEMS: FOUR SHORT CASES

Case 1. Sue: rower making a comeback

Background

Sue, aged 27, had been a successful member of her national team up until two years prior to the onset of consultation work. She had competed at Olympic and World Championships and finished in the top six in the world in women's double sculls. After this career-best performance, she retired owing to a combination of injury, the retirement of her older partner, the negative influence of sporting politics and a desire to explore life outside elite sport. She had recently resumed serious training with a younger partner and they were both motivated by the idea of making the national team for the 1996 Olympics. Sue felt that her unfulfilled goal of an Olympic medal was still within reach. They were coached by James, a former men's eight coach. Sue sought counselling because she was frustrated that her training and racing performances had not matched past levels or assumed current potential.

Content

A total of eight sessions took place, some involving both rowers and coach, some the two rowers together and some the rowers individually. The work described here occurred at an individual session with Sue. She reported a poor performance at a recent regatta – 'I just wanted to get it over with and get home, I hated being there.' In order to explore this, Sue was asked to identify her best-ever performance at a major event and recall, in as much detail as possible, her thoughts, feelings and experiences of this event. These comments were recorded by the counsellor on a flip chart. The process was then repeated, this time for her worst performance. The list shown in Table 5.1A emerged.

Table 5.1A Sue's comments about her best and worst performances

Best performance (World Championships)	Worst performance (regatta)
Fun	Scared
Wanted to show how good we were	Fearful
Excited	Wanted to get it over with
Enjoyed proving the coaches wrong	Nervous
Boat just ran	Boat wouldn't go
Confident	Nightmare
Bouncy	

Reversal theory interpretation

Her description of the regatta and her experience of it, along with known background information, led to the conclusion that she was in a telic state throughout much of the event and that this was very different from her preferred experience of competition. Sue's experience at the above two events could be described in reversal theory terms as shown in Table 5.1B.

Table 5.1B A reversal theory interpretation of Sue's comments about her best and worst performances

Best performance (World Championships)	Worst performance (regatta)
Paratelic	Telic
High arousal	High arousal
Pleasant negativism	Unpleasant conformity
Low tension stress; junior partner in boat, so low felt significance in relation to race tactics	High tension stress; senior partner in boat, so high felt significance in relation to race tactics

The experience and qualities of her best performance suggested that Sue's optimal metamotivational state combination should include the paratelic and negativistic states.

Intervention strategy

Several options were available in order to help Sue strengthen her ability to ensure that these states were operative, including helping her identify the specific antecedents that led to the best performance state. In reversal theory terms, these factors form a paratelic confidence frame (Apter, 1982, 1989). The approach chosen was to use the psychosynthesis technique of 'as if' visualisation, which has previously been adapted to sporting contexts by Syer and Connolly (1984). Sue was first asked if she knew of a rower who consistently exhibited the qualities and level of performance associated with her best performance. Sue was able to identify a Canadian international who embodied such an ideal model. Sue was then asked to close her eyes and physically relax before beginning a session of guided mental imagery. The first step was to imagine watching the rower and seeing her express the strength, confidence and technical expertise of an ideal performance. Once this image was clearly established, Sue was then asked to imagine herself becoming the rower so that she was experiencing the performance herself, from a perspective inside the Canadian. Finally Sue 'became herself' rowing and performing in this way. The imagery technique was used to give Sue confidence and induce the paratelic state and a protective frame.

Outcomes

Future work with Sue would have continued along the lines described earlier – concentrating on identifying the specific antecedents of the confidence frame that supported the ideal paratelic performance state. A combination of events led to the crew being excluded from national team selection and their coach moved to a men's crew, so Sue's return to competition was unfortunately short-lived. She did, however, report more enjoyment of training sessions and improved boat run after the work described here, so there was at least a subjective improvement in performance.

Case 2. John: arousal-seeking slalom canoeist

Background

John, aged 23, was an up-and-coming performer who had recently made the transition from a reserve to being a regular member of the national team. He narrowly missed selection in 1992 and 1993, then made selection in 1994 and 1995. His elder brother had been on the team for a number of years and had competed at Olympic level. John was nevertheless a very competent performer, finishing in the top ten of the World Cup rankings in 1994. His approach to racing was clearly paratelic: he enjoyed the buzz of racing and compared being on the start-line of a major race to surfing and seeing a big wave coming: 'You just think, "Yeah".' In the off-season he pursued high-arousal pastimes such as snow-boarding, surfing and off-road motorcycling.

Content

At the end of 1994, John wanted to begin a formal mental training programme. A performance profile (Butler and Hardy, 1992) was used to help him identify priority areas for improvement and this led to a focus on improved planning and confidence at major races. His experience was that, while he normally enjoyed racing, at major events he would feel less confident, somewhat more nervous rather than excited, and he would often compare his own standard unfavourably with that of more established competitors. When asked to describe the differences he perceived between himself and his rivals, John identified the important points shown in Table 5.2.

When John was asked what stopped him from being this way, his response was that he was concerned that if he were to become more like his competitors, he would lose the flair and spontaneity that characterised his performances and that he would find slalom less enjoyable.

Table 5.2 John's perception of the differences between himself and established competitors

Established competitors:
seemed to be more serious;
seemed to plan their training more carefully;
remained focused throughout the event;
were more consistent throughout the season.

Reversal theory interpretation

From a reversal theory perspective, John is a paratelic-dominant individual whose main motivation for participation in sport included the excitement and challenge of participation. At local races, where he was an established competitor, he was able to maintain the paratelic state owing to his familiarity with the conditions, the relatively low felt significance of the event and the low threat to his status should he fail to perform. In international events, particularly as a new member of the national team, he was less able consistently to maintain the paratelic state and was more likely to reverse to the telic state. This was due to the increased importance of the events and greater-than-normal frequency of comparisons with others. The telic state was unfamiliar for him and a less pleasant experience than his normal 'laid-back' attitude, so his performances suffered.

Intervention strategy

First, John's belief that being well organised and able to plan training were mutually exclusive of flair and passion was gently challenged by asking him to consider the example of a well-respected paddler who was able to exhibit both attributes appropriately. This drew on cognitive approaches such as Rational Emotive Therapy (Ellis, 1962, 1970) and was designed to open up for John the possibility of greater fluidity of metamotivational reversals.

Second, and following in a similar cognitive vein, attention was drawn to John's behaviour of self-evaluation and comparison with others. The consequences of this seemed to be a greater likelihood of an inappropriate telic state and increased nervousness. When John became aware of this pattern, he was more able to self-regulate himself – in his own words, 'I realised I just had to stop comparing myself to the other guys, it's so simple but I never realised.'

In order to help John experience an appropriate telic state, particularly during preparation for training, he was educated in the warming-up process developed by Syer and Connolly (1984). By systematically paying attention to the environmental conditions, oneself, coaches and other paddlers and, finally, the purpose of the training session, an athlete is able to develop greater presence and concentration during training or racing. John was encouraged to develop his own approach to this process and to ensure that training sessions remained enjoyable.

The final aspect was for John to make increased use of video replay of his own good performances. When watching himself, he was instructed, first of all, to imagine he was an objective observer and notice just how good he himself was. At the same time, he was to study technical aspects of his own performance to establish what were his strengths and any areas of weaknesses. These observations were used to design subsequent training sessions to address weaknesses. Finally, the video was to be used as an aid to visualisation of good performances. The use of video in this way was intended to strengthen John's ability to maintain the paratelic state during competition through increased acceptance of his own ability level, thus reducing the chance of unfavourable comparisons with others.

Outcomes

At the time of writing, the 1995 season was only just under way but John reported increased confidence through the early races. His description of the early season suggested that he had been able to maintain his familiar paratelic state at more important events. He felt excited and confident rather than anxious at the team selection races and produced his best-ever performance. Work was to continue through the season and would concentrate on identifying any additional factors that needed to be developed for John to maintain his preferred state at all events.

Case 3. Mike: professional pool player

Background

Mike, aged 24, was a talented amateur who was determined to make his career within professional pool (eight-ball). He ran his own pool hall and the game was a central theme to his life. By his own description he was 'very ambitious'. He began mental training work with the counsellor two months before he was due to turn professional and enter the top level of national competition. He already had a well-established pre-competition routine which involved a period of relaxation in a hot bath and subsequently increasing levels of focus and arousal as the match approached. Normally he felt 'psyched up' for a match and enjoyed the feeling of anticipation and 'nerves'. He reported that in recent tournaments he would typically start well and establish a good lead only to lose concentration, and often the match, when 'the voices started up'. This internal dialogue included comments to himself about the importance of the match, warnings not to miss the next shot, or fears about the prospect of losing. For example: 'This is a really important shot, you can win if you sink this ball.'

Content

The occurrence of intrusive or negative self-talk is common in sport and, while there is evidence that in some cases it helps performance (Van Raalte *et al.*, 1994), it is often considered by sport psychologists and athletes themselves to be a 'problem' that interferes with correct attention and concentration. In this case, rather than employ a cognitive–behavioural technique such as thought stopping, it was decided to offer Mike the opportunity of exploring the voices and discovering what they might have to offer. This was based on the hypothesis that the voice was that of one of Mike's sub-personalities (psychosynthesis; Assagioli, 1969, 1990) that had unique needs and, indeed, unique contributions to make to his performance.

Mike was asked to sit in a chair and spend a few moments recalling the type of self-talk he heard in a recent tournament, along with the tone of voice, feelings and thoughts associated with this experience. He was then asked to speak out loud the thoughts he had, addressing an empty chair that represented the 'Mike' who was busy playing pool. The sub-personality that emerged was serious, result oriented and wanted to win at any cost, playing safely and conservatively in order to do so. Mike was then asked to change chairs and identify with the 'Mike' who was playing. In stark contrast, this sub-personality was excited by the prospect of entertaining the crowd with spectacular, if risky, shots even if this meant losing the match. Mike named the first sub-personality 'winner' and the second 'showman'.

The 'chairs' and 'voices' procedure was a device or prop which allowed Mike to free-associate or role-play in an attempt to untangle internal conflicts. Work continued using chair dialogues and imagery to further explore these two sub-personalities. It emerged that the winner was prepared to do lots of boring practice and was motivated by the prospect of long-term success. The showman functioned almost exclusively 'in the zone' of high arousal and concentration and looked forward to the 'buzz' of competition.

Reversal theory interpretation

From a reversal theory perspective, it seems these two sub-personalities each represented a particular aspect of Mike's experience. Table 5.3 illustrates the attributes of each.

Table 5.3 Mike's likely operative states as winner or showman

Winner	Showman
Telic	Paratelic
Conformist	Negativistic
Autic	Autic
Mastery	Mastery

The winner was conformist in that he followed the accepted rules of the game and the normal or expected behaviour associated with it. The showman, however, enjoyed the opportunity to play radical shots and challenge the norms of conservative play. The lack of concentration could, in fact, be construed as representative of inappropriate reversals between the telic and paratelic states during competition. It was necessary to return to psychosynthesis to find a way of supporting appropriate metamotivational states, and hence appropriate attention, affect and cognition, during competition.

Mike's two inner selves seemed to have contradictory needs. To play conservatively may have suited the winner and helped to get an important result, but this often meant playing 'for safety' and resulted in a slow, sometimes tedious game that left the showman bored and unsatisfied. Yet to play purely as the showman was spectacular and entertaining for the crowd, but at the same time there was the distinct risk of losing the game. Through a process of dialogue and negotiation between the winner and the showman, Mike was able to discover and make explicit the needs of each sub-personality. Essentially, the needs were directly related to the free expression of the inherent qualities of each sub-personality. This process allowed each sub-personality to receive what he needed and at the same time clarify what each had to offer in support of their mutual aim – that of a successful career in professional pool. For example, the showman contributed flair and passion, the winner the ability to plan and analyse, with each coming to the fore at the most appropriate moment.

Intervention strategy

One strategy was for time to be set aside for exhibition matches in which the showman could be 'let off the lead'. Additionally, Mike decided to develop a tournament strategy in which he would initially play as the winner until the result of the match was beyond doubt then allow the showman to impress the crowd. Imagery was used to work towards the identification of another sub-personality, the 'professional', who expressed a combination of the winner and the showman. The professional could be flashy and precise together, choosing between and integrating the two alternatives.

Other work focused on strategies for improved practice sessions. While the winner was able to motivate Mike towards long and often lonely practice sessions, once engaged in practice the showman would come into focus. This suggested a telic to paratelic reversal during practice. When the showman was prominent and Mike was in a paratelic state of high arousal, practice involved lots of fast potting 'in the zone' of high concentration. For the showman, this was a preferred and exclusive state. By contrast, the winner could be in the zone or out; when out of 'the zone' he was analytical and saw the overall shape of a match. However, the winner was uncomfortable with these transitions, and when in the zone he was worried about leaving it because of fears that he would not be able to re-enter.

Mike's normal practice failed to replicate the real demands of a match because he preferred to stay at the table for long periods practising fast and difficult shots. In a match, there are often occasions when a player is forced to stand back and watch his opponent. This presents difficulties, because, if he is in the paratelic state, either arousal may drop and lead to unpleasant boredom or else a telic reversal may occur and lead to the high arousal being construed as unpleasant nerves. The solution was to introduce such transitions to and from the table into practice sessions so that Mike was more easily able to move between appropriate metamotivational states and sub-personalities.

Outcomes

Immediately following the early sessions in which the winner and showman were identified, Mike produced some of his best-ever performances, beating the reigning world champion. Work with this player continued and he continued to integrate more effectively the different aspects of himself. The voices during matches have been much reduced and Mike is now able to appreciate them for what they offer rather than see them as a distraction.

This case study provides evidence to support Kerr's (1993) contention that successful performance may require fluid and appropriate reversals between metamotivational states. In Mike's case, the primary axis of change was between telic and paratelic states, although there may also be some movement between conformity and negativism. The application of therapeutic techniques from psychosynthesis provided a means whereby such reversal could be facilitated by the athlete himself.

Case 4. Sarah: 'I don't much like myself when I'm a winner'

Background

Sarah was in her mid-twenties, bright, educated to degree level, and an international-standard competitor in her sport of slalom canoeing. She was ranked third nationally and was a top ten finisher in major World Cup events.

She performed best on difficult white-water courses where her boat-handling skills shone. Outside her main sport, she enjoyed surfing, mountain biking, rock climbing and 'hanging out with friends'. She was well liked, but until recently had not always been taken seriously as a competitor. She was very successful as a junior, winning a medal in the Junior World Championships when only 14, but then not really 'fulfilling her potential' in the eyes of others for several years. The transition to the senior team had been hard, and she was on the fringe for several years. The two national athletes ranked ahead of her had been members of the national team for at least four years and had achieved major international success.

Content

A particular issue was her relationship with the two team members 'ahead of her'. She felt uncomfortable focusing her training on beating them and disliked overtly competitive sessions. She preferred to concentrate on improving her own performance levels and competence, yet she knew that comparisons with others were unavoidable and necessary.

Mental training with Sarah started in 1994. The main focus was on helping her establish 'process goals' to improve the quality of her training and racing. These goals were carefully developed to help her concentrate on aspects of her performance that were under her own control and to avoid direct comparisons with others. The intention was to help her bring more focus and seriousness to her training without losing her great sense of enjoyment and spontaneity. At the same time, this helped her to develop a stronger sense of confidence and competence that was not only based on comparisons with her teammates. Her performance at races improved dramatically and she consistently performed at the top of her ability level.

She narrowly missed qualification for the 1996 Olympics. Prompted by this disappointment, she questioned her participation in competitive sport. In her own words, 'I've learned what I have to do to race well, but I don't much like myself when I'm a winner.' On further prompting, she explained that to be a good competitor she felt she needed to be selfish, self-centred and 'not a very nice person'. Her definition of a nice person was one who was thoughtful, sensitive and generous. These were qualities she did not associate with being a successful international competitor, where instead one 'needed' to be hard, demanding support rather than giving, and focused on one's own needs to the exclusion of others.

Reversal theory interpretation

Sarah is clearly paratelic–conformist dominant, evidenced by her lifestyle and recreation choices. She is probably also alloic–sympathy dominant, and therefore felt uncomfortable spending long periods of time in the autic–mastery state combination required by competitive sport.

Intervention strategy

The intervention at this stage consisted of helping her to reframe the qualities she associated with being successful, so that the positive aspects were also recognised – for example, being determined rather than greedy. Extensive emphasis on process goals was used to convert Sarah's dislike of comparisons with others in competition to an intra-autic focus (Apter, 1988) which concentrated on improvements in her own performance. Also, it was pointed out to her that everyone is capable of expressing many different qualities in different aspects of their lives, so to be a particular way in one context did not necessarily mean that one was like that in all contexts. There were many ways of expressing the qualities of a 'nice' person that did not compromise the expression of other qualities in a sporting context, and vice versa.

Outcomes

Sarah spent a two-week holiday with her boyfriend, camping and surfing in Scotland, before returning to training and competition with renewed enthusiasm. She then decided to become involved in sporting politics as an athlete representative, where she works to improve funding and support for her own and other sports. Sarah also got involved with charity work, where she felt she was helping others and contributing to a more just society (alloic–sympathy). She found a way of enjoying sport and developing her considerable talent by increasing her range of life experiences to include more metamotivational state combinations, especially the alloic domain that was squeezed out of her life as more time and attention went on training and competing. The sporting politics and charity activities made her feel better about her participation in sport and, in reversal theory terms, brought an element of balance to her metamotivational experience (see Figure 5.1).

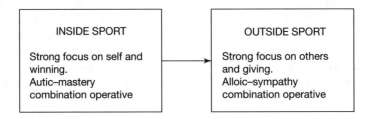

Figure 5.1 Maintaining balance in Sarah's metamotivational experience by inducing reversals through her involvement in charity and other work outside sport.

FURTHER COMMENT ON THE FOUR CASES

The case studies presented above help to illustrate how elements of other counselling or psychotherapeutic approaches can be used within the eclectic approach of reversal theory. In this regard, reversal theory has been shown to be compatible with humanistic methodologies such as psychosynthesis, as well as more mainstream cognitive–behavioural interventions. The main advantage offered by this eclectic approach is that reversal theory provides an encompassing model of motivation and emotion that is based on the athlete's individual experience of sport.

It should already be apparent from what has been said previously that athletes should be able to recognise their preferred performance state combination and endeavour to perform with that combination operative. This may well involve the use of performance routines in an attempt to make pre-competitive behaviour and thinking consistent as a means of inducing preferred states and maintaining high levels of performance. However, one of the basic notions of reversal theory is that human behaviour is inherently inconsistent. This applies equally to athletes and, while perhaps difficult to deal with at the applied level, means that athletes and coaches must be ready to respond to any inconsistencies in an athlete's behaviour. Occasionally, athletes may even find themselves operating well in a non-preferred state combination, as illustrated by the following example.

Exceptional Olympic performance

Mary Peters was competing in the pentathlon high jump event of the 1974 Olympic Games. All the other events, with the exception of the men's pole vault taking place at the other end of the stadium, had finished. She had outjumped all her opponents and, under floodlights and cheered on by some 50,000 spectators waving Union Jacks and chanting her name, she jumped higher than she had ever done before.

> I have never been so emotionally involved with a crowd. I so badly wanted to give them back some of the love and encouragement they were giving me that I found myself doing incredible, extrovert things that had never entered my head before. I was coming out of the pit and kicking my heels up like a foal. I was running down to the edge of the track to blow kisses to a particularly noisy bunch of British spectators. Each time the tears were welling up in my eyes until all I could see of them was a watery blur. I have seen it all on television films many times since and, each time, I simply cannot believe it is me . . . it was completely out of character. . . . For me, at the end of a day of enormous tension and physical strain, an overwhelming desire to give more and more for my coach and my team manager and those marvellous supporters who had come halfway across Europe was pushing me onwards and upwards.
>
> (Peters and Woolridge, 1974, p. 83)

From this description, the intensity of her feelings for the other people around her is clearly related to the alloic state, and her desire to perform well for them to an alloic–mastery state combination. However, these were unusual feelings for her. As she herself states, 'there had been occasions in the past when I had completed a pentathlon high jump without a solitary spectator in sight' (Peters and Woolridge, 1974, p. 82). Athletes may find themselves with metamotivational states operative which are not part of their customary, preferred metamotivational pattern when competing. In Mary Peters' case, her unusual emotional experience allowed her to perform beyond her expectations in the high jump and win the pentathlon gold medal after the final two events on the next day.

Mary Peters' experience in the 1974 Olympic Games was truly exceptional. Based on evidence from both qualitative and quantitative research findings from reversal theory studies (e.g. Males and Kerr, 1996; Wilson and Kerr, 1999; Males *et al.*, 1998; Purcell, 1999) and counselling work with athletes (e.g. Males, 1995, 1996), the accepted wisdom among those working with reversal theory and sport is that athletes will generally perform best with their preferred performance metamotivational state combination operative. However, athletes should remain psychologically flexible and be prepared to work with or deal with reversals which may occur at any time prior to or during performance. In addition, athletes may vary in their ability to initiate conditions which are likely to induce reversals and there will be individual differences in metamotivation and susceptibility to reversal (lability) (Apter, 1989). As a consequence, some athletes may simply reverse more easily or more often than others.

COGNITIVE RESTRUCTURING AND GUIDED IMAGERY IN REVERSAL INDUCTION

Kerr (1993, 1997) argued that if athletes received the correct psychological training, they could use strategies such as cognitive restructuring or imagery to induce reversals. Also, in recent years a variety of techniques for inducing reversals, including self-conditioning, ritual, role-playing and imaging, have been taught by Michael Apter in his company workshops (Apter International).

In addition, on the basis of the results of their work in stress management and counselling work, Fontana and Valente (1997a) point out that cognitive therapies generally provide an individual with a reasonable level of direct control over their motivation and mood. They also state:

> the present authors' counseling experience (particularly in dramatherapy) suggests that people can indeed think themselves into a particular role and quickly acquire the metamotivational state to accompany it. This is perhaps still technically involuntary, but it certainly comes close to being voluntary in that the cognitive processes are under voluntary control, no input is required from the environment, and reversal may be accomplished almost instantaneously. The whole thing may be accomplished so effortlessly that there is a sense in which effectively, and for all practical purposes, the process is voluntary.
>
> (p. 207)

This is encouraging for those who might wish to use cognitive restructuring to induce reversals in sport situations.

Recently, Doug Perkins and George Wilson, working at the University of Tasmania, set out to test the usefulness of imagery for inducing reversals. In a research study, they investigated the relationship between elevated physiological and felt arousal, emotion, metamotivational state, and performance on a strength task in elite athletes (Perkins *et al.*, 2001). The athletes were recruited from sports which generally demand maximal motor activity over short time periods (e.g. track-and-field throwing and sprinting events). A custom-designed inventory was constructed to measure the emotional state of the athletes during the experiment. It included the Telic State Measure (TSM; Svebak and Murgatroyd, 1985), visual analogue scales (VAS) to assess hedonic tone and emotional strength of imagery, and rating scales from the Tension and Effort Stress Inventory (TESI; Svebak, 1993) for measuring anxiety, relaxation, excitement and boredom. Telic dominance was also measured.

In the first session, the athletes were interviewed on tape to obtain personal experiential data for use in developing two personalised scripts (one an arousing telic experience and one an arousing paratelic experience) which were to be used later in guided imagery format. Presented below are two examples of the personalised scripts used in the research.

Telic script: participant no. 28

> Close your eyes and imagine back to November last year just before the state all-schools championships are to be held up at the Domain. You have been training in preparation doing 60 metre sprints and on the way home and that night you can feel that not all is right with your hamstrings. I want you to really put yourself back in this situation [pause]. You don't really want to admit it but something is wrong – when you stretch your hamstring out you can feel pain. The next day is just horrible as you try to hide what has happened. You go to training but you arrive early and finish before anyone else comes. You are feeling really lousy about that. That night you go to bed without really eating much and you feel really tense. Here you are in about the best form of your high-jumping career – last week you broke the state record – but now you may not be able to compete. Really try to imagine your feelings now [pause]. Not only that, your mum has bought you new high-jump spikes and you feel like maybe you're letting her down a bit if you don't get to jump. You can't sleep – you are feeling really tense. You toss and turn and feel all knotted up and you can't handle this. At about 1.30 in the morning you go and tell your mum about your injury – you feel horrible.

Paratelic script: participant no. 20

> Close your eyes and picture yourself at the Penguin ground at the start of the year. It's a sunny Saturday afternoon. You're competing in the high jump. I want you to really put yourself back in this situation [pause]. While waiting to come into the competition you notice how unusually high the mat is stacked behind the bar. You come into the competition after the bar has been raised and you are feeling good and your first few jumps have been good ones. Your

coach is there and is letting you know how well you are going. Every jump is making you feel good and you seem to be jumping better and better. You are jumping higher than you have ever done before and you think, 'How come I haven't jumped this high before?' It's quite amazing and it's giving you a real buzz. Really try to imagine your feelings now [pause]. Everything feels as though it is going just right. You are not concentrating hard, you are simply enjoying the sensation of jumping. This feeling is great and continues as you go on and win. You've never jumped better and you take the buzz into your next event, the 400. Your run is also a great effort. You are feeling really positive. You're having a great day.

In the second session, athletes took part in the experiment individually. Electrodes connected to physiological recording equipment were attached to each seated athlete. After baseline measurements had been taken, athletes were asked to close their eyes, maintain breathing to pacing tones (set at either 10 or 20 breaths per minute) and listen to the 60 to 80 second script presented over an intercom system by the experimenters, situated in an adjoining room. When the script was finished, the athletes opened their eyes and took the dynamometer (placed down by their side) in their dominant hand and squeezed it as smoothly and hard as they could for three or four seconds. Immediately after this, they completed the custom-designed psychological inventory. This procedure was repeated individually with each athlete for telic, paratelic and neutral scripts (containing twenty common nouns and used as a control), with script and respiration rate order counterbalanced. Athletes were allowed a short break between each experimental condition.

The results showed that psychological factors, rather than physiological factors, were important in the performance of hand grip strength. Changes in physiological arousal were not associated with performance. However, using guided imagery for manipulating felt arousal and metamotivational state (telic–paratelic) produced significant increases in autonomic activity, hedonic tone and emotional intensity. The best strength performance was obtained with high felt arousal and high hedonic tone in the paratelic condition. These results not only confirm Kerr's (1993) argument that imagery could be used to induce reversals, but, more importantly, also provide scientific justification for its use in counselling work with athletes. In the cases of Sue and Mike, presented at the beginning of this chapter, imagery was being used in counselling sessions to treat their problems with inappropriate reversals. The results of Perkins et al. (2001) suggest that guided imagery could also work effectively to induce reversals at the competition site. The short duration of the scripts and the fact that an appropriate personalised script could be presented by a coach or the athlete him or herself, via an audio tape on a Walkman-type player, make it feasible. These results are promising, but further investigations focusing on athletes at the competition site will be necessary to confirm the usefulness of guided imagery for inducing reversals to athletes' preferred performance metamotivational state pattern.

CLOSING COMMENTS

This chapter has examined short-term performance motivation problems in four short cases. Salient in Sue, John and Mike's performance problems were different difficulties concerning the somatic states (telic, paratelic, conformist, negativistic). In contrast, salient in Sarah's performance problems were the transactional states (autic, alloic, mastery, sympathy). These cases illustrate the eclectic nature of the reversal theory approach to counselling athletes. Each case was different, and the subsequent counselling sessions used a number of intervention techniques, yet each counselling strategy was based on reversal theory principles. As mentioned earlier in this book, reversal theory's eclectic approach is rather like a computer operating system on which many software programs could be managed and used even more effectively. How this works in practice has been demonstrated by the case study material presented in this chapter.

In each case, the intervention was formulated around the athlete's preferred state combination for competitive sport. As with Mike, the pool player, the preferred state combination may be different in different types of competition or even within different stages or parts of the same competition. Also, it may be that an athlete's overall metamotivational state dominance is at odds with the preferred performance state combination. Where this occurs, the reversal theory sport psychologist needs to help the athlete develop and/or adapt well-defined strategies which assist him or her in tolerating these states long enough to perform well.

The following chapter will examine longer-term performance motivation problems brought about by athletes being 'forced', because of their particular circumstances, to operate in the same metamotivational state or state combination for long periods of time, giving rise to tension stress. This stress arises from structural disturbances to their motivational experience brought about by inhibited reversals (Murgatroyd and Apter, 1984, 1986).

SUGGESTED FURTHER READING

Kerr, J. H. (1993) 'An eclectic approach to psychological interventions in sport: reversal theory', *The Sport Psychologist* 7: 400–418.

Kerr, J. H. (1997) *Motivation and Emotion in Sport: Reversal Theory*, Hove: Psychology Press.

Males, J. R. (1999) 'Individual experience in slalom canoeing', in J. H. Kerr (ed.) *Experiencing Sport: Reversal Theory*, Chichester: Wiley.

FOR DISCUSSION

Mark: confused triathlete

Interested in triathlon, Mark, aged 25, is the fourth fastest in his country and is ranked in the top sixty in the world. His current goal is to gain a place in his national team and make it to the next Olympics. He trains twenty hours a week, but feels that this is inadequate, even though his job is flexible and designed to fit around his training. He can't relax until he has done his set training programme for the day. He very rarely goes out or has a drink and does nothing that will affect his training. He feels that he is always in control of his anxiety and always feels calm before a race. He puts this down to experience and knowing that he has prepared well. In one recent top event, he set specific goals for the swim, but not the other parts of the race. He did well on the swim section, achieving his goal. The result was that he found himself well ahead of the main pack while on the bike. However, the bike pack caught him very quickly and then managed to drop him equally quickly. Mark felt that he just didn't have it in him to keep up with the pack. He was not sure why, because he had been doing well and they were not that fast. Rather than fall so far behind, he became despondent, dismounted and walked back to the transition area, which was very embarrassing because everyone was watching. He had a tough time dealing with this race, both during and after. He could not explain his mood and was frightened that it would happen again.

Mark consults you, as a sport psychologist, about his performance problem.

1 What do you think happened to Mark during the race?
2 How would you attempt to counsel him using the eclectic approach of reversal theory?

Bill: top performer with a problem

Bill is a paratelic-dominant elite water sport athlete who managed some excellent performances last year, including a top-two place at the world championship. He is technically and physically very talented. He enjoyed the buzz of this experience and there was little inter-personal threat from or to the other competitors. In fact, Bill said he was often inspired by his competitors' good performances, describing major international races as 'like running up a wall to see who can reach the highest', a paratelic–conformist–autic–mastery state combination. This year, in spite of last year's excellent performances, he missed out on national team selection, where eight athletes competed for only four places. Bill described the national team selection as 'very intense and unpleasant; I like the other guys, I don't want to put them out of the team'. Now his performances are poor; he misses the team and spends his time just playing at his sport and going surfing.

1 Think about the possible reason for Bill's remark about the national team selection event, after he performed so well in the world championship. What were the likely metamotivational state combinations involved, and why was the national team selection event unpleasant and stressful for Bill?

2 What factors would be important in any type of intervention strategy which might help Bill get 'back on track'?

Chapter 6

Athletes experiencing stress

INTRODUCTION

Athletes may encounter long-term and stressful performance motivation problems associated with their training and competitive environments. The first case study reported below focuses on paratelic tension stress as experienced by Dave, a professional soccer player who had close contact with the author for a period of four years.

DAVE: BORED SOCCER PLAYER

Background

Dave, a 30-year-old male professional soccer player, had been playing professional soccer for twelve years for two different professional teams in a European country. He came from a large family, and his father and brothers also played soccer (one brother professionally). Dave first became involved in soccer at the age of 6, when he joined the club where his brothers were already playing. He was not pushed or forced to play soccer by his father or brothers, but joined of his own free will. When he was 7, he began to play competitive soccer for his club and school teams. Later, as a teenager, he progressed to his city youth team where, while playing against other city and district teams, he was scouted by the coach of 'Newtown', a professional team. Dave accepted the coach's invitation to join and moved to the junior ranks of the professional game.

Injuries to members of the Newtown third team resulted in a fairly rapid promotion from the juniors to the third team, where he played well and retained his place in the team for the remainder of his first season. Still playing well in the next season, he progressed to the second team and even played a few games for the first team. He was then 18 years old. By the following year he was a permanent member of the first team and went on to play for them for a total of ten years. Newtown was reasonably successful, in one season finishing fourth in the National Premier Division, thus qualifying for a place in one of the European soccer tournaments.

However, it was more usual for the team to finish the season in the bottom half of the national premier division and they were relegated to a lower division twice in the period in which Dave played. In the early days of his career, attracted by the challenge of playing with more talented players in front of more spectators, Dave's ambition was to play for one of the top clubs in the country.

It was during the latter part of Dave's time with this team that the author first became acquainted with him and, through informal conversations, learned that Dave was generally not enjoying his soccer. After a few months, the author asked Dave (then 26) if he could interview him about his experiences in professional soccer, and Dave agreed. The interview followed a semi-structured format and was recorded on audiotape. Following the first interview, Dave completed the Telic Dominance Scale (TDS; Murgatroyd *et al.*, 1978), which was subsequently scored and showed Dave to be paratelic dominant.

After ten years, Dave realised his ambition and was transferred to 'Redfield', one of the top teams in his country. In his first year, Redfield finished third in the National Premier League and, in the second year, qualified for European competition. Even so, after two years of playing well and receiving a high salary, Dave, to the surprise of the manager, players and supporters, announced his intention to leave the club. He left his home country to start a new life with his female partner in a foreign country.

Why would a professional sportsman, at the top of his profession, make such a decision? It was to pinpoint the reasons why Dave, then 30 years old, had decided to leave Redfield that a second semi-structured interview was conducted. The results of the two interviews are summarised below.

Interview 1

Dave pointed out that the playing and training schedule for professional soccer players was extremely demanding. He usually had only one free day in the week, Wednesday. On other days he trained in the afternoon. In addition, he often played two games a week. In Europe, although soccer is a winter sport, the summer break is only six weeks long, and even less for some players if their team does well and has to play in the national cup final.

From his answers to the author's questions, it became apparent that in the early days, Dave thought of soccer as fun and he was not primarily concerned with financial reward. He was happy to be playing in the top division and thought of the money he received as a kind of bonus or extra. He felt that playing well was more important than money. However, Dave's experience had changed over the years and, as a senior player, much of this fun element seemed to have disappeared. He was not the only player to feel this way. Dave described how, within the Newtown team, there were two groups, one comprising older players (aged approximately 26–29 years) and one made up of younger players (aged approximately 19–20 years). According to Dave, most of the older players felt the same way he did: they were becoming tired of soccer and most felt they had to play too often.

In answer to the question, 'Do you think by being a professional and training and playing so often that some of the fun has gone out of the game for you?', Dave replied:

> I think so. It's an obligation. Every time on the park the crowd's watching you and when you make a mistake you read it the next day in the paper. The next time you play there is a lot of pressure on you and I don't like that. When I was young (18 or 19) everything was OK, but now, I'm playing better than then, but sometimes I get worse criticism. You have to become better and better.

When not playing or training, Dave's fellow players spent much of their free time playing snooker, billiards or cards and watching videos (according to Dave, largely in an effort to counteract periods of boredom). Dave was one of the few in the Newtown professional club to continue his education. He passed the necessary exams and was accepted for study at a college of physical education, eventually graduating as a fully qualified physical education teacher. He was then able to combine playing professional soccer with part-time teaching. This he found both physically and psychologically demanding.

Interview 2

In this interview, Dave talked about his initial enthusiasm about the transfer from Newtown to Redfield. Towards the end, he had become unhappy with Newtown. He thought that the club organisation was amateurish and management repeatedly sold the best players to other clubs, making it difficult to build a good team. He felt as if he had seen it all before and he was not getting much satisfaction any more. He thought that Redfield was a more professional organisation and had looked forward to the change of environment and the new challenge of playing with one of the top teams in the premier league. Also, his salary at Redfield was higher.

In spite of his enthusiasm at the time of his transfer, it appeared that, even with a new club, Dave found the psychological demands of training and playing so often, problematic:

> I loved training, especially for the exercise. But with soccer six or seven times a week, the practices were always the same. That can get very boring. I noticed with a change of activity, playing a different sport or skipping a training session, the excitement and pleasure came back.

To the question 'How did you feel when playing competitive games?', Dave replied:

> At 18, playing for the first time in the first team, I was very tense and nervous. Suddenly you are playing with star players who you'd always admired. The

highest you could reach. You played for the game and not for the money. I saw it more as a hobby. After playing more and more games and getting older, the pleasure faded and I saw it more as a job, as an obligation no one enjoyed. Sometimes I felt like it, sometimes I didn't.

In addition, Dave gave the main reasons for his decision to leave Redfield:

I never was an ideal soccer player. Soccer was not my whole world. My social life was very important to me; I frequently went to bars and parties. Because of this, the club did not know whether to extend my contract, despite good results and the fact I played every game during the two years I played for them. The second reason was that I had had enough of top soccer. Football gets boring, meeting the same opponents every time, sitting in a bus all the time.

By this time, Dave, who continued to teach part-time, was looking for a full-time job as a physical education teacher. In addition, a serious relationship had developed between Dave and his female partner, who lived in a different European country. They decided that they wanted to be together. Had Dave's feelings about his soccer situation been different, she would have moved to his country. In the circumstances, however, they decided to move to her country. Dave had lived in his own country for thirty years and he felt that 'to live and play soccer in a different country was attractive'.

The final question of the second interview was very specific, as was Dave's answer. 'How big a factor in your decision to leave Redfield was boredom and the lack of excitement?'

If you want to become a good soccer player and play at the highest level and you do everything to accomplish that, then you have a rather boring life. Sleeping, eating, training, travelling and playing controls your life. Soccer decides everything. Only in the summer you have four weeks off, the rest of the year you have to be at their disposal. You cannot go away for the weekend. Your life is lived for you; press, fans. It can be fun, but in general it is very annoying.

Reversal theory interpretation

Dave was shown to be paratelic dominant by his TDS results, a finding that was confirmed by, for example, his comments about his social life and the importance of going to bars and parties, places where there would be plenty of action and he could experience the high arousal and excitement that paratelic-dominant individuals enjoy. As Martin *et al.* (1987) have shown, paratelic-dominant people are susceptible to paratelic tension stress if their lives do not present them with sufficient 'stressors' (problems, difficulties and crises to be overcome).

Paratelic-dominant people thrive on environmental demands, especially if increases in demand result in high felt arousal. Although not the only way to achieve high hedonic tone in the paratelic state, stressors certainly are one of the important factors for achieving this for paratelic-dominant people.

Dave highlighted a number of features of professional soccer which he considered contributed to increasing levels of boredom as his career proceeded. These included aspects of playing and training (performing the same practices, playing against the same opponents, playing too many games), aspects of travelling to games and other aspects of preparation for games. Over time, this repetitive, dull routine became increasingly at odds with his paratelic-dominant personality and the variety, challenge and excitement that he thrived on. He wanted soccer to provide the paratelic high felt arousal thrills and excitement that he had experienced during his early career. However, his predominant experience in his latter seasons was one of paratelic low arousal characterised by boredom and tension stress. In addition to feelings of boredom, Dave also indicated some annoyance about how being a professional soccer player meant relinquishing a large degree of control over his own life. Soccer dictated what he could do and when he could do it. These feelings of a lack of control over his own life would also have contributed to Dave's tension stress, but they would have been associated with the transactional states rather than the paratelic state.

It is clear from both interviews that Dave's soccer experience had changed over the years. At the beginning of his career, his soccer experience was essentially paratelic in orientation. He relished the opportunity to play professional soccer, happy to be doing something he enjoyed and not too concerned with financial gain. Training and playing were pleasant and he enjoyed the challenge of trying to establish himself permanently in the team.

However, the challenge of soccer did not seem to be sufficient for Dave's paratelic-oriented personality. He had a certain amount of free time, but rather than engage in the same 'time-killing' activities as his colleagues (playing snooker or watching videos, for example), he set himself the extra challenge of following a teacher education course. This new challenge of first studying and later teaching young people can be seen as an attempt to help offset some of the paratelic tension stress he was then experiencing as a professional soccer player.

As the thrills of actually playing the game diminished over the years, Dave's attempts to set up new and interesting challenges (for example, through teaching and his social life) not only involved greater and greater investment of paratelic effort stress, but also became less and less effective in coping with boredom. As a result, even though Dave was at the top of his profession and performing very well, paratelic tension stress associated with soccer had built up to levels that were so uncomfortable and so unpleasant that he decided to stop playing. The pleasure and challenge of living with his foreign partner on a permanent basis and the challenges associated with living in a foreign country were more attractive than continuing to invest large amounts of effort stress in a battle with paratelic tension stress and boredom.

It should be noted that the interpretation presented here is not intended to suggest that Dave would have been experiencing paratelic tension stress all the time. One of the basic premises of reversal theory is that people do reverse between different pairs of metamotivational states fairly frequently. Dave's tension stress was specifically concerned with his experience of training and playing soccer. Indeed, if Dave could have reversed more often in the telic-oriented soccer context, much of his tension stress might have been resolved. A reversal to the telic state would have resulted in unpleasant boredom being replaced by pleasant relaxation. Also, even in the latter part of his career, his emotion-focused efforts to cope – for example, through distraction and socialising with friends – would have been at least partially successful. Consequently, it was not in all aspects of his life that Dave experienced this form of stress. In soccer, Dave's problem was brought about by inappropriate levels of felt arousal in his operative state and/or by too often being in the wrong operative state for the telic-oriented soccer environment.

Intervention strategy

In spite of his difficulties, at no time did Dave consult a sport psychologist or even discuss his feelings with the club management, who were unaware of his difficulties. With the cooperation of the Redfield coach and manager, it might have been possible to change Dave's attitude to training and playing and to have extended his time in professional soccer. Any form of reversal theory-based intervention (Kerr, 1993, 1997) with a chance of being successful would have had to take into account his paratelic-dominant personality, addressed his need for new and different challenges, and allowed for a greater degree of personal control in his life. For example, Dave's paratelic tension stress might have been reduced by a change in the telic-oriented training climate to include new and different activities. While these changes to training might have helped, it is unlikely that they would have been totally successful in dissipating Dave's feelings of stress. What Dave, as a senior player, needed was a less regimented, more flexible approach to training and playing (e.g. Curry, 1992). Coaching staff, for example, might have been persuaded to allow him to occasionally engage in some other type of demanding sport in place of training. Encouraging him to engage in other sport activities would have allowed Dave to achieve and enjoy high levels of felt arousal, which might have proved successful in offsetting stress effects. For example, participation in risk sport activities, such as parachuting or motor sport, has been shown to be preferred and enjoyed by paratelic dominant individuals (Kerr, 1991; Kerr and Svebak, 1989). In Dave's case these types of activities, or something similar, might have provided the extra challenge and high levels of arousal that he, as a paratelic-dominant individual, frequently needed.

Dropout or burnout?

One final question arises regarding Dave's motivation problem and his eventual exit from soccer. Did he drop out or burn out? There has been research carried out on these two phenomena. Briefly, Petlichkoff (1996) reviewed the results of studies carried out over two decades which examined dropout from youth sport. Among the reasons cited by young people from these studies for dropping out were that it was 'too boring', they were 'not having fun' and they had 'other things to do'. These reasons would seem to be very similar to comments made by Dave. Gould and his colleagues (Gould *et al.*, 1996a, b, 1997) examined burnout in junior tennis players in considerable detail. In the first of these papers the authors summarised a list of situational demands associated with athlete burnout which were gleaned from studies completed prior to 1996. This list of situational demands included lack of control, excessive time demands, limited social relationships, restrictive parental involvement, inconsistent or negative feedback from coaches, repetitive training loads, and high volume of competitions. Several of these situational demands are also reflected in Dave's comments.

Braman (1996), in a paper entitled 'The role of response satiation in overtraining and burnout in sports', not only traced the history of burnout (and related concepts which pre-dated it) in psychology (e.g. Hull, 1943; Pavlov, 1926/1960; Sechenov, 1863/1965), but also linked it to reversal theory. This paper is so important to understanding burnout and dropout in sport that it is included in this volume as an appendix (pp. 129–143). However, for present purposes, the distinction between dropout and burnout is neatly summed up by this statement by Braman (personal communication, 27 June 1996) and leads to the conclusion that Dave did not burn out, but dropped out of soccer:

> The reason burnout has interested me for so many years is that it is so paradoxical. The person is excited and loves what he is doing, and the signs of burnout come before he has any subjective loss of enthusiasm for the undertaking. Your example of a paratelic-dominant athlete whose coach is 'making work out of the sport', and therefore ceases to enjoy it, and therefore quits the sport is NOT paradoxical. The paratelic-dominant athlete who quits a sport because it has become too telic and just plain boring, drops out, he does not burn out. People who give up an activity because it is no longer rewarding are simply manifesting extinction; this is not paradoxical, mystifying nor particularly interesting. What is interesting, mystifying and paradoxical is the person who LOVES the activity yet finds himself unable to continue it, the person who 'burns out'.

OTHER FORMS OF TENSION STRESS

Tension stress results in uncomfortable, uneasy feelings associated with the experience of unpleasant somatic and transactional emotions (boredom, anxiety, anger, sullenness, humiliation, shame, resentment and guilt) (Apter, 1997; and see Chapter 1). This tension is greatest when the mismatch between felt and preferred levels of a metamotivational variable, such as felt transactional outcome, is greatest. Conversely, when felt and preferred levels of the variable are close to equivalent, the athlete is at ease and experiences one of the eight pleasant emotions (excitement, relaxation, placidity, provocativeness, modesty, pride, virtue, gratitude). Remember, tension stress can be reduced either by changing the level of the metamotivational variable concerned, or by reversing to the partner metamotivational state.

The case from soccer focused mainly on the tension stress associated with the telic and paratelic states, but tension stress can also arise from problems associated with any of the other pairs of states. In the transactional states, for example, tension stress can also occur as an outcome of an athlete's interaction with family, friends, coach or fellow athletes (e.g. the lack of control element in Dave's experience). This is illustrated more powerfully in the next case, which involves Jenny, an acrobatic skier who experienced tension stress associated with the transactional emotion, resentment.

JENNY: NEGLECTED ACROBATIC SKIER

In the past, freestyle skiing encompassed three disciplines: acrobatic, mogul and aerial skiing. The individual disciplines have now become so specialised that each has emerged as an individual sport in its own right. Jenny's first appearance in the national acrobatic skiing championship resulted in her finishing in tenth place. She was 19 years old and still enjoyed acrobatic skiing just for fun, as a recreational sport. Two years later she finished in fifth place in the nationals and started training with a coach who concentrated on the technical aspects of her flips and jumps and improving her physical condition. During the following year she became a member of the national team, but broke her leg in a fall. It took six months to heal. While recovering from injury, she set herself the goal of becoming an Olympian. Once her leg was rehabilitated, she continued to improve and two years later, aged 24, she became national champion and competed for the first time on the World Cup circuit. Here her best result was ninth. She felt that she was in heaven, competing with athletes she had previously seen only on videotape. At this early stage, she thought of herself as just a challenger and felt that there was nothing to fear as far as results were concerned. As it happened, her results were good, as they were again in the World Cup the following year.

Still national champion, she competed in the Albertville Olympic games in 1990. At Albertville things started to go wrong and she was very disappointed with her performance. After the competition she was so furious with herself that, back in her room, she hammered and kicked the door, beds and other furniture. That year her World Cup results were also extremely poor. She became aware that the coach was paying a great deal of attention to an 18-year-old teammate, where previously, as the newcomer, Jenny had been the centre of the coach's attention. Increasingly, she felt the coach had lost interest in her and began to feel isolated.

During the next year, she made mistakes and fell at almost every contest in the World Cup, finishing well outside the top ten. She also lost her place as national champion. She began to feel that she could no longer perform well and had lost a lot of her previous confidence. She felt increasingly resentful and complained about the poor judges, incompetent organisers and her own bad luck. Although her performance improved slightly during the next year and she regained number one position in the national rankings, she felt that she could no longer trust the coach and continued to feel under pressure from her 'up-and-coming' rival, who remained the coach's favourite, receiving 90 per cent of his attention and leaving the remaining 10 per cent to be split among the rest of the team. The year was full of stress for Jenny, to the extent that, for the first time, she hardly enjoyed her skiing.

Jenny had planned that the final event in her career would be at the Lillehammer Olympics in the following year. As it turned out, however, the acrobatic skiing event was excluded in 1994 and her chance to make up for her poor performance in Albertville was lost. Jenny continued to feel that the coach was taking no real interest in her and, although she complained, nothing changed. He claimed that he treated everyone the same, but in reality he still favoured one girl and gave little advice to Jenny, the senior member of the team. She was left to work things out for herself. Much of the time she was angry or depressed and her feeling of being persecuted became steadily worse. In terms of performance and personal satisfaction, it was an extremely low point in her career.

Reversal theory interpretation

It is perhaps hard to believe that the poor relationship between Jenny and her coach could have endured for so long. However, athletes sometimes have to put up with this kind of situation when a coach has a well-entrenched position in a sport (e.g. Ryan, 1996). As Jenny was an elite athlete, training and performing occupied an important part of her life, including constant association with her coach and teammates. In terms of felt transactional outcome in her interactions with coach and rival athlete, Jenny experienced the sense of loss and poor hedonic tone associated with tension stress in the autic–sympathy state combination. In terms of emotions, her resentment towards the coach and her young rival increased steadily over the years.

As shown in Figure 6.1, if Jenny's coach had radically changed his behaviour and paid more attention to her, it might have resulted in feelings of felt transactional gain. She would then have experienced pleasant feelings of gratitude, rather than resentment, towards her coach. If Jenny could have become more team oriented,

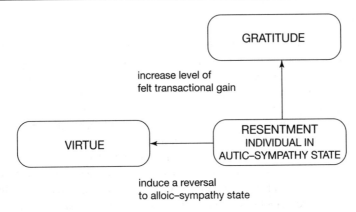

Figure 6.1 Possible changes in state combination and felt transactional outcome, affecting Jenny's relationship with her coach and young teammate.

or if her young rival had perhaps looked up to Jenny and sought her advice from time to time (as the most experienced member of the team), it might have caused Jenny to reverse to the alloic–sympathy state combination and resulted in feelings of virtue rather than resentment.

This interpretation of Jenny's case has obviously been simplified in order to illustrate one particular example of tension stress arising from the transactional emotion, resentment. It is quite likely that she could also have experienced other forms of tension stress during this period, as different forms of tension stress can coexist over the same time frame (Apter, 1997). For example, during the low point in her career in 1994 after the Lillehammer Olympics, she also experienced anger and possibly anxiety, in addition to resentment.

However, it should also not be forgotten that in any problem relationship, the people concerned often have very different perceptions about the relationship and it is always useful to hear 'both sides of the story'. Although not possible in this case, it would have been interesting to have heard her coach's version of his relationship with Jenny. Of course, he may well have favoured the younger athlete, but he probably would not have seen the relationship the same way and would have had a rational explanation for his behaviour. He may, for example, have thought that Jenny was a whiner, or an undisciplined athlete who had difficulty in controlling her temper, or an athlete who had fulfilled her potential and who now was 'over the hill'. While reversals to an alloic–sympathy state combination would have been beneficial, so too might a more conventional cognitive–behavioural intervention that would have helped Jenny re-examine her attitudes and expectations about her coach and herself. It was very probably not just the coach's behaviour that blocked the necessary reversals, but Jenny's own beliefs and attitudes about herself. In fact, her experience at a Canadian training camp, described below, did just that, so that when she returned her attitudes and confidence were improved.

Postscript

Jenny did not consult a sport psychologist about her performance motivation problem, but near the end of 1994 she found someone from the acrobatic ski world, a former US men's champion, with whom she could talk extensively about her difficulties. She found that this helped her a great deal. The following summer Jenny joined a training camp which he organised in Canada. He started her thinking more about the artistic part of acrobatic skiing and she also successfully tried some new jump techniques that she had wanted to learn. In effect, he became a substitute for her coach, and Jenny's interaction with him made up for what was missing from her interaction with her coach. She was able to experience pride at mastering the new techniques and gratitude towards her new mentor for his help and advice. The tension stress and strong feelings of resentment were eased, at least temporarily. When she returned to competition, her coach's attitude had not changed, but Jenny found that her confidence had returned and what she had learned from the training camp worked well. Also, even though many other skiers fell during their descents, she herself did not fall, remained calm and stopped complaining about the conditions on the ski slope. She found that she was enjoying skiing again. She competed successfully for the next few years, regaining and holding the national championship and improving her World Cup results. At the Nagano World Championship she put in her lifetime-best performance, just missing a medal.

CLOSING COMMENTS

The purpose of this chapter has been to show how athletes may face longer-term performance motivation problems as a result of a build-up of tension stress. A build-up of tension stress may be caused by factors within their training and competitive environments. The cases of Dave and Jenny illustrate two forms of tension stress arising from very different sources and different metamotivational state combinations and emotions. In Dave's case, the dull routine and rather inflexible conditions that he experienced within soccer brought about tension stress arising from the somatic states and emotions. In Jenny's case, difficulties in her interactions with her coach and some of her fellow skiers manifested themselves in tension stress related to the transactional states and emotions. Dave's problem remained unresolved until he quit soccer in his home country. For Jenny, a chance meeting and some sound help and advice from a sympathetic fellow athlete 'turned her around' and she was able to compete again successfully.

Another long-term performance motivation problem forms the central theme of the next chapter. Here the outcome of being 'locked' in a certain state or state combination as a result of *reversal inhibition* can be very serious for the athlete. Indeed, if this type of performance motivation problem becomes severe enough, an athlete's psychological and physical health could well be at risk. Those most at risk are young athletes, especially females, in sports which require extremely long hours of hard training, such as swimming, gymnastics and ice skating. However, adults are not exempt from these risks, especially in endurance sports such as long-distance running, cycling and triathlon.

SUGGESTED FURTHER READING

Braman, O. R. (1996) 'The role of response satiation in overtraining and burnout in sports', paper presented at the First International Workshop on Motivation and Emotion in Sport: Reversal Theory, Tsukuba, Japan, October. (See the Appendix.)
Kerr, J. H. (1997) 'Over the top? Stress in competitive sports', in J. H. Kerr, *Motivation and Emotion in Sport: Reversal theory*, Hove: Psychology Press.
Svebak, S. and Apter, M. J. (1997) *Stress and Health: A Reversal Theory Perspective*, Washington, DC: Taylor and Francis.

FOR DISCUSSION

University rugby in Japan is much like American football in US universities: games are highly competitive, the top games attract large numbers of spectators and, after university, the best players go on to further their careers with company teams (the equivalent of US professional football). Kohei Fujii was a very talented prop forward in the Tsukuba University rugby union team. (When asked, following the interview, if he would allow part of the contents to be published anonymously, Kohei readily agreed, but insisted that his real name be included.). At 16 years of age, he started playing rugby at high school, practising six days a week, one hour or so per session. The coach was not tough and the training was easy. When Kohei went to university, he got a severe shock because training there was also six days a week, but for two and a half hours per session. In addition, he often did fitness activities such as weight training, running and swimming. He sometimes had free time in the afternoon, but could never feel at ease, worrying about the next training session.

As a freshman, Kohei's first match in the 1st XV was on an overseas tour to the Netherlands and England. After this, bent on improving his performance, he steadily developed into a skilful and competitive player who had a successful career in the Tsukuba team. He was scouted by one of Japan's top company teams. The author interviewed him, using a semi-structured approach, in March 1999, just after he announced his ultimate decision to decline their invitation and stop playing rugby altogether. His replies to some of the questions asked during the interview follow:

(a) his best memory during his university rugby career:

For me it was the intensive forward training every Wednesday. The training was so hard that I couldn't stop myself from almost vomiting every time.

Although I hated the training, it made the scrum much stronger, and I became more experienced. Now, I feel the training was important in developing my play.

(b) his best experience in a match:

The Tsukuba versus Waseda matches in '97 and '98. In the '97 match, I was able to beat my opponent. He had defeated me in the past, but this time (the third time) I trained hard so that I could defeat him and finally made it. In the '98 match I scored a try for the first time. When I scored the try and got applause from the crowd, I felt a bit embarrassed because it was really unusual for me. I think about games in terms of my personal role, my individual contests.

(c) his favourite part of rugby:

Because of intensive training, the team's scrum has become strong, and has had a good reputation. As for me, I am not good at other plays, so I concentrate on the scrum and don't want to be defeated by other opponents. Now that we have real ability in the scrum I am dying to scrum down. The scrum is the highlight of the game for my position.

(d) his role as a team member:

Not only because of the training, but also because of the many other jobs, being a Tsukuba University rugby player is a full-time commitment. In the team, I have to do many things which I don't want to, and I got tired of doing such things. I can bear the hard physical training, but not the mental exhaustion. Sometimes we had unexpected meetings where we had to watch match videos so many times. These kind of things made me really tired.

(e) turning down the opportunity to join a company team:

I recognised my limitations, I was burned out. I had worried about it for a long time, thought it through over and over again and finally made a decision not to go.

(f) what he would do instead:

I want to be a fisherman. Watching a TV programme, I became fascinated by fishing. In the programme, one fisherman living in Okinawa caught a big spearfish. My home town in Gifu prefecture has no sea, and I want to live in a place where I can see the sea all the time. At the beginning, I wanted to be a fisherman half as a joke, but now I'm serious. Another reason to be a fisherman is that a fisherman can do his job by himself, or with a few people at most. He is responsible for himself. There's no need to be part of an organisation with many people, and to do things I don't want to. I am not rebellious, but the job as a fisherman, the individuality, has an attraction for me. While pelagic fishing needs a large number of people, coastal fishing just needs one family or so with a small boat. That is why I prefer coastal fishing.

After leaving university, Kohei did become a fisherman and now has plans to become a firefighter. He no longer plays rugby.

1   What would Kohei's likely operative metamotivational state combination have been for much of his time at university? Why was it difficult for him to experience other state combinations?
2   Would this have resulted in Kohei being subject to tension stress and, if so, what type(s) of tension stress would he have experienced?
3   If Kohei had consulted you, as a reversal theory sport psychologist, during his playing career, what would you have advised him to do to prevent his subsequent feeling of being burned out?

Chapter 7

Reversal inhibition and inappropriate strategies in athletes

INTRODUCTION

As can be seen from the material presented in Chapter 6, the experience of stress can have a detrimental effect on performance motivation over the long term. Another long-term difficulty can arise as a result of a reversal process problem known as *reversal inhibition*. Reversal inhibition occurs when an athlete becomes 'locked' or 'trapped' in a certain state or state combination and experiences great difficulty in reversing (Kerr, 1993). If it endures over time, it may seriously affect an athlete's psychological and physical health.

JUDY: MASTERS ATHLETE

Judy is a 35-year-old Asian markets stockbroker and averages sixty to seventy hours at work per week. Her job is fast-paced and stressful in the sense that she has to watch the fluctuations of the financial world, often concentrating on several changing situations at the same time, and make crucial decisions within a very short time-span. Judy is also a successful masters athlete who competes against other women in her age group. She started exercising at the age of 28, after never having done any exercise or sport activities. She decided that she *had* to complete a marathon before she was 30. Without seeking advice from anyone, she put together her own training plan, and although in the beginning she could run only 100 metres at a time, completed her first marathon as planned, before she was 30.

On top of her work, she puts in eighteen to twenty hours of weekly training. This takes place as early as 4.00 or 5.00 a.m., as well as at lunchtime and in the evening. Judy says that 'she lives for training'. She never misses her training sessions and, if she is injured, she just continues training. She has even been known to cancel important work appointments to get her training completed. If for any reason she has a poor training session, she then trains twice as hard the next time. For Judy, every training session is critical and has a specific goal. She worries about not achieving these goals. She also describes herself as never feeling like taking things easy and always having to be busy, even when she is at home. When she goes on holiday, she always has to have a definite purpose and typically goes hiking in the mountains or attends a training camp. Judy rarely goes out socially and follows fairly strict rules about drinking and diet.

Reversal theory interpretation

Most reversal theorists would recognise that Judy exhibits what Apter and Svebak (1984) described as a Type A/telic behaviour pattern. Characteristics of the Type A behaviour pattern include speed, impatience, competitiveness and hostility (e.g. Chesney *et al.*, 1981). In the Type A/telic behaviour pattern, these characteristics are combined with the usual characteristics of people in the telic state (serious, planned, goal and future oriented). It should be obvious that Judy's participation in sport is really just an extension of her Type A/telic behaviour at work and her lifestyle in general.

First, consider the fact that she chooses to participate in an endurance sport. Svebak and Kerr (1989) established a link between certain types of sport and telic- or paratelic-dominant lifestyles. They found that telic-dominant athletes typically participated in endurance sports such as cycling, long-distance running or rowing, involving repetitive, monotonous activity, while paratelic-dominant athletes typically participated in explosive sports such as baseball, basketball, cricket, soccer, involving spontaneous, impulsive, explosive action.

Second, much of Judy's time is spent in the telic and conformist states. Certainly, her whole training regime, as described above, suggests that when she is training and competing, the telic and conformist states are operative. In addition, Judy, working as a stockbroker in a man's world as well as training and competing to the extent that she does, is also likely to have the autic and mastery states operative for much of her daily life. Indeed, Judy exhibits all the signs of reversal inhibition and being trapped in a state combination of telic–conformist–autic–mastery in which the telic state may be salient. It seems that she has few, if any, opportunities for reversing to any of the respective partner states. Even when at home or on holiday, times which might well have afforded possibilities for reversal in other athletes, Judy still feels the need to accomplish things ('never feels like taking it easy').

In reversal theory terms, individuals exhibiting inappropriate reversals, reversal inhibition or any of the other three inappropriate strategies for achieving satisfaction in a state (to be discussed later in this chapter) are considered to be psychologically unhealthy (Apter, 1989; Lafreniere *et al.*, 2001). Taking into account metamotivational dominance, individuals are considered psychologically healthy if they:

1 can reverse with some frequency between metamotivational states;
2 have the appropriate states operative for their social environment and their own needs;

3   can achieve satisfaction in those states without causing distress in other
     people;
4   can achieve satisfaction in those states without creating difficulties for future
     reversals or the achievement of satisfaction.

In other words, to be psychologically healthy, individuals' or athletes' lives require
a degree of instability or flexibility rather than enduring rigidity. Judy may well
have difficulty satisfying criteria 1 and 4 above and therefore, according to reversal
theory, would be considered psychologically unhealthy. As a result, her physical
health may also be at risk. At face value, she appears to be a healthy athlete who
enjoys and gets satisfaction from participating in her sport. Further consideration,
however, suggests that there are several features of her sporting activity which
could be a cause for concern with regard to her psychological and physical health.
Her single-minded, perhaps obsessive, dedication to completing regular training
three times per day, and the fact that she says that she 'lives for training', continues
to train even when injured, and feels the need to compensate for a bad training
session in her next outing, are indicators of possible exercise dependence (Veale,
1995; Kerr, 1997). A second worrying fact is that she has strict rules about drinking
and diet, which might also be an early indication that the development of an
associated eating disorder is a possibility. Brief details from a reversal theory-based
research study on exercise dependence and eating disorders in triathletes are
considered important in this context and are included in the next section.

REVERSAL THEORY RESEARCH ON EXERCISE
DEPENDENCE AND EATING DISORDERS

There is a growing research literature on exercise dependence and exercise
dependence related to eating disorders (e.g. Pierce, 1994). Some recent studies
(e.g. Bamber *et al.*, 2000) have begun to address the distinction made by de
Coverly Veale (1987) between primary exercise dependence, where exercise
dependence exists independently, and secondary exercise dependence, where
exercise dependence is associated with some form of eating disorder. One of these
studies (Blaydon *et al.*, forthcoming) examined the metamotivational characteristics of eating-disordered and exercise-dependent athletes.

The participants in the study were 203 male and female triathletes, a mixture of
elite and sub-elite, amateur and professional. They each completed the Exercise
Dependence Questionnaire (EDQ; Ogden *et al.*, 1997), the Eating Attitudes Test
(EAT; Garner and Garfinkel, 1979) and the Motivational Style Profile (MSP; Apter
et al., 1998). MSP results indicated that triathletes were generally telic, conformity,
autic and mastery dominant. Female triathletes were found to be significantly more
telic and mastery dominant than males.

The triathletes in the study were also divided into professional and amateur
groups, and further analysis of MSP scores revealed that professionals were

PRIMARY EXERCISE DEPENDENCE	SECONDARY EXERCISE DEPENDENCE
High EDQ scores Low EAT scores	High EDQ scores High EAT scores
EATING DISORDER ONLY	NO DISORDER/EXERCISE DEPENDENCE
Low EDQ scores High EAT scores	Low EDQ scores Low EAT scores

Figure 7.1 The characteristics of the four independent groups identified by Blaydon *et al.* (forthcoming).

significantly more telic, autic and mastery dominant than amateur triathletes. Analysis of the EDQ and EAT questionnaire responses indicated the presence of four separate groups: a primary exercise dependence group; a secondary exercise dependence group; an eating disorder only group; and a group with no exercise dependence or eating disorder (see Figure 7.1).

Examining the MSP results of these four groups also indicated that professional primary and secondary exercise-dependent triathletes were more telic, conformity and autic dominant than professionals in the other two groups, thus suggesting that the dominance profile of the professional primary and secondary exercise-dependent triathletes may have played a role in the development of their exercise dependence. In contrast, the amateur secondary exercise dependence and eating disorder groups exhibited similar dominance profiles, with significantly higher telic, arousal avoidance, negativism and mastery dominance scores than the other two amateur groups. This result suggests that there might be a link between this dominance profile and the development of an eating disorder.

From the case material presented above, Judy's metamotivational style certainly matches that of the female triathletes in general; that is, Judy is telic, conformist, autic and mastery dominant. Although, as a stockbroker, she was not a professional triathlete (in terms of financial income criteria used to differentiate between triathletes in the study), she certainly appeared to be 'professional' in terms of her attitude and dedication to training and competing. In the study, results from the professionals showed that telic, conformist and autic dominances were important with respect to the development of exercise dependence. There is some evidence from these results which suggests that Judy might be exercise dependent.

Intervention strategy

As it happens, Judy has never consulted a sport psychologist, but if she, or any athlete with a similar reversal inhibition and likely exercise dependence problem, did ask for counselling, what type of reversal theory intervention might be attempted?

In Judy's case, counselling would not be easy, because it would appear that the reversal inhibition that she may well experience in sport may also pervade her everyday life. Therefore, to be effective, counselling might have to spill over to address lifestyle issues, rather than merely focus on her behaviour in sport. It would be important to help Judy to see her behaviour in sport and her exercise dependence in motivational terms so that she could gain some personal insight into her own experience. This would involve encouraging her to identify her motivational experiences and their structure and then to try to facilitate a change in how she experienced her motivation and actions (Lafreniere *et al.*, 2001). In addition, the psychologist's role would be one of generating more versatility in Judy's meta-motivational experience ('unlocking') by trying to facilitate reversals in all four metamotivational pairs. Of these, telic to paratelic state reversals might be first priority. The first steps might involve activities which are fun and the use of humour (Murgatroyd, 1981, 1987a), and an attempt to get her to carry a 'paratelic climate' over into her sport activities. Some examples might include training without a watch, which might prevent her from constantly evaluating times, running speed and training goals; concentrating on quality rather than quantity in training; and occasionally participating in other demanding sports for fun, but in risk or explosive sports rather than sports of an endurance type (Svebak and Kerr, 1989). Maintaining a 'here and now' focus (Murgatroyd, 1981) would also be important. This might be achieved by getting her to pay close attention to her bodily responses while training and adjusting accordingly. For example, the Scandinavian idea of 'fartlek' running, or running as you feel, could be proposed. Judy should ease up on training when her body feels stiff and tense, and train harder when her body feels supple and loose, and she is moving well. She should also definitely be encouraged to stop training when injured.

Incidentally, Svebak's research using electrodes and electromyographic recording instruments to record muscle tension graphically (Svebak 1984; Svebak *et al.*, 1982) is of related interest here. According to his results, when individuals were in the paratelic state, their electromyographic gradients were flatter than when they were in the telic state. To generalise these findings to sport, this means that athletes performing sport activities in the paratelic state are likely to become fatigued less rapidly, perform better because they are not tensing up, and have fewer injuries than when performing in the telic state (Braathen and Svebak, 1990).

A sport psychologist should also try to provoke some negativistic behaviour in Judy by encouraging her not to stick to training goals religiously and to just do something different and unplanned in training, or to skip training sessions occasionally (especially if she has started to replace quantity with quality). In addition, a sport psychologist would do well to examine the nature of Judy's social relations. Getting her to train together with a training partner, or as part of a group of athletes, might help to induce reversals from the autic and mastery states to the alloic and sympathy states, which in turn might help to shift the focus of her attention from herself to other athletes from time to time, as might more social outings in general.

Judy rarely goes out socially, but taking part in non-serious social outings in a group might also help to promote reversals within metamotivational pairs.

YOUNG ATHLETES AT RISK

In sports such as gymnastics, swimming and ice skating, young athletes are often at risk of developing physical or psychological (or a combination of physical and psychological) health-related problems. Female athletes in these sports must, of necessity, start at a very early age because those who are successful will often be performing at the highest levels in their early teens. For these athletes, driven on by fanatical coaches and over-zealous parents, the long hours of extraordinarily demanding and dangerous training take an enormous toll on young bodies and minds. Ryan (1996, p. 3), surprised by what she found during her research into young female gymnasts and skaters, pulled no punches when she said:

> What I found was a story about legal, even celebrated, child abuse. In the dark troughs along the road to the Olympics lay the bodies of the girls who stumbled on the way, broken by the work, pressure and humiliation.

The brief case histories of Mayuki and Susan, two young female swimmers, in countries on two different continents thousands of miles apart, illustrate the kind of problems that Ryan (1996) identified.

Mayuki and Susan: a tale of two swimmers

Mayuki, a Japanese girl, started swimming when she was just 4 years old. She had developed asthma as a result of an allergy and her parents took her to a local swimming club, thinking that swimming might help her breathing. She grew to like swimming and turned out to be one of the best swimmers in the club, beating most of the other swimmers in the different strokes. By the age of 7 she was training seriously and taking part in the national junior championships, specialising in the 50 metre butterfly. Training for Mayuki was tough. She completed an hour and a half's training before school and the same in the evening after school. By the time she reached 14, the daily training load had been increased and further supplemented by an extra three hours on Saturdays and Sundays. She was now training or competing seven days a week. She stopped menstruating.

The next year, feeling negativistic and rebellious about her whole life being dominated by swimming, Mayuki decided to quit. She particularly wanted to study hard to gain entrance to a good senior high school. As her times were still improving, her coach disapproved of her decision to stop. He told her that studying was unimportant and that she should continue training and competing. Her parents and teammates approved of her decision because they had seen the coach abandon other swimmers whose times had stopped improving. Mayuki felt that she could not trust her coach and decided to work and plan towards her future. She passed the high school entrance examination and was happy with her success, so much so that she voluntarily returned to swimming with her old coach a few months later. However, her performance had deteriorated and, when it showed no signs of improving, the coach told her to quit so that he could concentrate on another swimmer. This selfish but, in the case of this coach, typical behaviour left her feeling sad and angry about attempting a comeback, and about swimming in general.

Susan was also 4 years old when she started her career in competitive swimming in England. Her career progressed until, aged 16, she became a nationally ranked swimmer for the 100 metre breaststroke, competing in various national and international events. By the time she reached secondary school, her training routine was especially long and hard. Her typical day started at 5.30 a.m. with two hours of training with the swimming squad. She did strength training during the school lunch break, in addition to doing cross-country running and playing netball for the school teams. After school she had to study and try to complete her school work before training for a further two to three hours in the evening with the swimming squad. She usually clocked up in the region of 80 to 100 kilometres per week, which is not unusual for full-time athletes in competitive swimming. Two years later, however, when Susan was 18, she was diagnosed with overtraining syndrome. Doctors told her that her white blood cell count was so low that any minor illness could have killed her. Susan was forced to retire, even though she firmly believed that she could become a top swimmer and this was important to her.

Susan put a lot of the blame for her forced retirement on her coach for not having read the signs earlier. Her weight had started to drop rapidly, which he said was good. He knew her periods had stopped, but avoided the subject. As a young swimmer, Susan had put her complete trust in the coach. All she wanted to do was please him by improving and, when she failed to do so, she worked even harder than he asked. He was an up-and-coming coach who could only see potential glory and was therefore a real task-master who did not really understand the importance of rest. It took Susan three years to recover her health. She too subsequently tried to make a comeback but, like Mayuki, realised how far she had fallen behind and gave up.

Reversal theory interpretation

Leaving aside the question of damage to Susan's physical health for the moment, how can we explain the psychological effects of this type of prolonged and intensive training, in reversal theory terms? The task for Mayuki and Susan at each training session was to complete the programme of pool lengths, swimming at different speeds and using various strokes and training aids, prescribed by their respective coaches. Both athletes were young females being coached by authoritarian male coaches whose single-minded objective was to produce winning swimmers at the highest level. Given these conditions, it would be fair to say that during training, the athletes' predominant metamotivational state combination would have been telic–conformist (all Susan wanted to do was please her coach by improving).

On top of this, the preoccupation in these training sessions with perfecting their individual techniques, personal best times and comparison with other swimmers in their club or group strongly suggests that the other element in their predominant metamotivational state combination would have been autic–mastery. The whole climate of swim training forced Mayuki and Susan to have a specific state combination operative for several hours a day, every day. In addition, after early morning training they were attending school, where they were also expected to be serious about work and conform to school discipline and rules. Improving their knowledge in the different subjects would also have been a priority. Some activities may well have been group rather than individually oriented, but certainly, unlike other girls of similar age, Mayuki and Susan would have had fewer opportunities to have fun in the paratelic state, be negativistic, or interact with their friends and family in the alloic and sympathy states. As a result, over time, these two athletes could have lost the balance or equilibrium in their metamotivational experience and become prone to developing reversal inhibition. In other words, Mayuki and Susan could have become trapped in a telic–conformist–autic–mastery state combination.

As it turned out, Mayuki retained enough metamotivational versatility to eventually rebel and go against her coach's wishes, determining to do her own thing and pursue her own activities. Susan persevered to the point that she became physically ill and was forced to retire from swimming early. She was fortunate that doctors discovered her low white blood cell count before she contracted any kind of illness. In discussing Susan's very serious medical problem, it should also be mentioned here that young females, like Mayuki and Susan, in sports where body weight and shape are crucial to success, are also very much at risk of developing eating disorders. Ryan (1996), for example, documents the considerable problem of anorexia and other eating disorders among young gymnasts and skaters. In the case of top US gymnast Christy Henrich, the eating disorders she developed while competing proved fatal. She died at the age of 22.

INAPPROPRIATE STRATEGIES

Reversal inhibition and inappropriate reversals (discussed in Chapter 5) are different forms of structural disturbance in motivational experience between partner states and constitute two of the five forms of psychological disorder identified by reversal theory. Beyond these two, there are three further disorders which make up a second category known as *inappropriate strategies*. These are *functionally inappropriate*, *temporally inappropriate* and *socially inappropriate* strategies and are concerned with problems associated with trying to achieve satisfaction (or avoid dissatisfaction) *within* a state (Apter, 1989; Lafreniere *et al.*, 2001; Murgatroyd, 1987b; Murgatroyd and Apter, 1984, 1986) (see Figure 7.2).

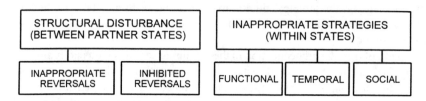

Figure 7.2 The five forms of mental disorder identified within reversal theory (after Apter 1989).

Athletes exhibiting functionally inappropriate strategies are likely to be in the appropriate states at appropriate times, but the strategies are likely to produce a different, or even opposite, effect than that which was actually intended (Lafreniere *et al.*, 2001). For example, a male athlete in the telic state who is continually anxious about completing training regimes and achieving performance goals in competition, and who worries that this anxiety is not helpful to his performance, is subject to a functionally inappropriate strategy. Worrying about his anxiety is not helpful. In fact, it serves to compound his anxiety problem, reducing his chances of personal achievement and thus his gaining satisfaction in the telic state.

Temporally inappropriate strategies occur when an athlete, in order to avoid unpleasant feelings and distress in a particular state or state combination, employs strategies which provide immediate pleasure or satisfaction, but which make it more difficult to avoid the distress in the future. For example, some athletes may satisfy their needs through the immediate gratification that comes from activities such as gambling, drug or alcohol abuse, or sexual promiscuity. Here the states in question are likely to be the paratelic and negativistic states and, if the paratelic–negativistic-oriented activity continues, over the long term it may develop into a much more serious problem (e.g. drug, alcohol or gambling addiction). Alan Merson, Tony Adams and Paul Gascoigne are three English soccer players who may have been subject to temporally inappropriate strategies which disturbed, or may have unbalanced the structure of their motivational experience. All three were international players who had a drinking problem which led to alcoholism, affected their play and threatened their careers. Following drying-out and rehabilitation, Merson, Adams and, perhaps to a lesser extent, Gascoigne have managed to come to terms with their alcoholism and rescue their athletic careers.

The third type are known as socially inappropriate strategies. Strategies are defined as socially inappropriate when the metamotivational state combination results in behaviour that, while satisfying the needs of an athlete, causes distress and suffering in others. A good example is when athletes become preoccupied with injuring opposing players, as in the violent stick attack by Boston Bruins ice hockey player Marty McSorley on Donald Brashear of the Vancouver Canucks in a match played in February 2000. The two players had twice fought earlier in the match, with Brashear getting the better of McSorley in the tussles. With only 2.7 seconds of the match left, McSorley, with a vicious swing of his hockey stick, struck Brashear a two-handed slash to the right temple, leaving Brashear, who fell and hit his head on the ice, lying unconscious. However, McSorley's violent action, which perhaps satisfied his own need to resolve his angry resentment, caused severe injury and distress to Brashear and outrage among players, the National Hockey League (NHL) authorities, the spectators at the match and the millions of people who watched the incident on television. He was banned for the remainder of the season by the NHL in what was the harshest penalty ever imposed on an ice hockey player. Later, in a Canadian court, he was found guilty of assault.

Any of these three types of inappropriate strategies may be combined with either of the structural disturbances (inappropriate and inhibited reversals) to form more complex conditions which Apter (1989) argues are the source of many well-recognised psychological disorders (e.g. chronic anxiety or depression, phobias; see Apter, 1989; Lafreniere *et al.*, 2001 for more details).

CLOSING COMMENTS

To deal with individuals who present problems associated with inappropriate reversals, inhibited reversals and inappropriate strategies, reversal theory advocates an eclectic approach to psychotherapy. Sport psychologists can benefit from an understanding of this approach, as the principles are central to any counselling based on reversal theory as a theoretical foundation. In the final chapter, which examines reversal theory's eclectic approach to therapy in detail, the focus shifts to some extent from the athlete to the sport psychologist. Important elements of this eclectic approach, including athlete problem assessment, intervention treatment and strategies, and the psychologist's own behaviour, are discussed.

SUGGESTED FURTHER READING

Kerr, J. H. (1997) *Motivation and Emotion in Sport: Reversal Theory*, Hove: Psychology Press.

Lafreniere, K. D., Ledgerwood, D. M. and Murgatroyd, S. J. (2001) 'Psychopathology, therapy and counselling', in M. J. Apter (ed.) *Motivational Lifestyles in Everyday Life: A Guide to Reversal Theory*, Washington, DC: American Psychological Association.

Apter, M. J. (1989) *Reversal Theory: Motivation, Emotion and Personality*, London: Routledge.

Swoap, R. A. and Murphy, S. M. (1995) 'Eating disorders and weight management in athletes', in S. M. Murphy (ed.) *Sport Psychology Interventions*, Champaign, IL: Human Kinetics.

Carr, C. M. and Murphy, S. M. (1995) 'Alcohol and drugs in sport', in S. M. Murphy (ed.) *Sport Psychology Interventions*, Champaign, IL: Human Kinetics.

FOR DISCUSSION

As a rugby union player, Brian had a physical build that was perfect for his position, and he was fast and immensely strong. He was very skilful. His passing was good, he could kick accurately with either foot and his tackling was fearless. In his early career, however, it looked as though his behaviour might be a hindrance to the development of his potential as a player. Brian despised authority and seemed to go out of his way to provoke trouble. He was expelled from school, one week before the end of the school year, for sending the headmaster a parcel – a shoebox containing excrement.

He later turned his dislike of authority to the committee members of his club team. At one stage, a directive came through from the Rugby Union about dangerous play, especially the kicking and raking of players on the ground in rucks. The club chairman and committee informed players that they would be treated severely if they were seen doing this in matches, even if the referee did not take action. In the very first match after this announcement, Brian kicked an opposing player in the back so badly that he was carried off the field injured. Not only did he injure the opposing player, but he did so right in front of the grandstand containing the chairman and other committee members. The referee missed the incident, but, true to their word, the committee suspended Brian for several matches. Also, the team had to travel frequently to matches and stay overnight in hotels. Brian often indulged himself in acts of vandalism, setting off fire alarms and letting off fire extinguishers in the middle of the night, damaging furniture and fittings in his room, raiding the kitchen and carrying out senseless acts such as stomping packages of honey and jam into the dining-room carpet. On one occasion he urinated into a plant pot in a busy hotel lobby. Much of this behaviour occurred when he had been drinking. During an overseas tour, Brian's behaviour was considered so reprehensible that he was banned from playing for the representative team for a considerable period. Brian enjoyed behaving in this fashion and thought that, even through they prevented him playing, the suspensions and punishments he received were lots of fun.

1   Was Brian's behaviour the result of a psychological problem or just a case of high spirits?
2   If you think it was a psychological problem, describe the nature of the problem in reversal theory terms.
3   On the basis of what you have read in this book so far, if Brian had come to you, as a sport psychologist, for counselling, how would you have tried to help him deal with his problem (that is, which type(s) of intervention would you have used and why)?

Chapter 8

The sport psychologist and eclectic athlete counselling

INTRODUCTION

In Chapter 5 the use of the reversal theory eclectic approach to athlete counselling was compared to a computer program manager system which increases the effectiveness of the person using the computer. In the same way, applying reversal theory to athlete counselling increases the effectiveness of the counsellor by, for example, providing a theoretical structure on which to base the choice of technique and implementation of an intervention. In relation to reversal theory's eclectic approach, it is worth noting that:

> It is often the case that the word 'eclecticism' is a euphemism for 'unsystematic' and 'uncritical' and that in therapy it represents a kind of 'anything goes' philosophy. It should, however, be evident that the structure provided by the reversal theory analysis which has been presented here is far from unsystematic and uncritical and is certainly not compatible with any old mish-mash of therapeutic techniques.
>
> (Apter, 1989, pp. 157–158)

If the application of reversal theory to work with athletes is to be effective, then there are certain skills which can facilitate psychologist–athlete interaction (Apter, 1989; Lafreniere *et al.*, 2001; Murgatroyd and Apter, 1984, 1986). It is the aim of this chapter to examine these skills and point out how they can assist the sport psychologist to deal with aspects of the reversal theory approach, such as athlete problem assessment, decision-making about intervention techniques and strategies, and the sport psychologist's own behaviour (Kerr, 1993).

ATHLETE PROBLEM ASSESSMENT

In several of the preceding chapters, case examples of the different reversal problems that athletes may encounter were examined and interventions discussed. In this process, however, it is essential for the sport psychologist not only to identify an athlete's problem, but also to gain an understanding of the way the problem is experienced and interpreted by the athlete in reversal theory terms. Problems must be reviewed phenomenologically to try to establish motives and metamotivational states operational during specific events and/or instances. Reversal theory requires us to be open-minded and not to prejudge behaviours, interpersonal transactions, use of drugs, or addictive behaviours, but to try to identify what the athlete was thinking and feeling and what he or she was trying to achieve. This can occur only if the psychologist has been able to establish a feeling of empathy and mutual trust with the athlete. When the athlete's experience is truly understood, the psychologist is in a position to make an informed decision about intervention strategy and treatment. If the psychologist fails to understand the true nature of the athlete's metamotivational experience, any intervention is likely to be ineffective and perhaps even counter-productive (Lafreniere et al., 2001).

Lazarus's (1981) BASIC-ID assessment format (behaviour, affective states, sensations, imagery, cognitions, interpersonal relations and drug-taking behaviour) can be utilised to build up case histories and guide the evaluation process. Murgatroyd and Apter (1986) have found this format useful in general psychotherapy, and Davies and West (1991) and Perna et al. (1995) for use in the counselling of athletes. There are also a number of reversal theory assessment tools that can assist in the process of assessment (Apter, 1989; Lafreniere et al., 2001). These include metamotivational state and dominance measures, which have been described in detail in Chapter 3, and the use of written description by the athlete in, for example, diary keeping (e.g. Chapter 4). Diary keeping can be pre-planned for specific times or can be triggered by, for example, pager signals. In addition, athletes can be asked to write up a situation analysis report in which they concentrate on situations which are crucial to their presenting problem. Later the psychologist and the athlete can explore these situations, focusing on operative states, reversal patterns and behaviour in the particular situations. Finally, careful use of simulation and drama therapy (Fontana and Valente, 1997b) can provide a safe environment in which the sport psychologist can evaluate his or her assessment of the athlete's reversal problem. The nature and intensity of simulation and drama therapy techniques mean that sport psychologists need to keep ethical considerations very much in mind when using them.

DECISION-MAKING ABOUT INTERVENTION TECHNIQUES AND STRATEGIES

Sport psychologists who base their work on reversal theory have the advantage of being able to choose from a number of different intervention strategies to achieve effective results. If one strategy fails, then a new strategy can be applied. For example, interventions with an athlete experiencing high levels of competition anxiety could focus on reducing arousal levels to more manageable levels or, alternatively, on the induction of reversals to the paratelic state, where the anxiety would be experienced as excitement. However, the psychologist has to consider each athlete and each situation carefully. Reducing levels of metamotivational variables such as arousal may not be effective in many competitive sport situations, but inducing reversals might prove very effective. In other sport competitive situations the opposite may be true: inducing reversals may prove ineffective, but reducing the level of a metamotivational variable may be just what is required. Furthermore, combining strategies may lead to undesired outcomes. For example, in the case of the athlete experiencing anxiety prior to competition, if arousal is reduced and reversal induction also takes place, the athlete may find him or herself in the paratelic state under low-arousal conditions experiencing boredom.

In the actual counselling sessions themselves, the operative state of the athlete client is important and may influence the choice of intervention strategy adopted by the sport psychologist. For example, counselling which focuses on the serious, long-term consequences of an athlete's behaviour is unlikely to succeed in producing the desired response in athletes with the paratelic state operative. Alternatively, exploring creative and novel solutions to athletes' problems is unlikely to be successful with athletes with the telic state operative who are unable to shift their focus from the serious nature of their problems (Lafreniere *et al.*, 2001). Getting the athlete into the paratelic state during counselling can be particularly useful as, with the establishment of a protective frame, an athlete may feel the confidence and protection necessary to engage in diverse and innovative techniques (Murgatroyd, 1981, 1987c).

Prior to engaging in counselling, it is advisable that a contract be made between the sport psychologist and the athlete client which clarifies both their roles, outlines the nature of the problem, explains the rationale for the planned intervention choice, and establishes evaluation procedures (Kerr, 1993).

BEHAVIOUR OF THE SUCCESSFUL THERAPIST

In counselling sessions, the choice of intervention technique may mean that the psychologist has to operate in particular metamotivational states or state combinations. Therefore, the sport psychologist who exhibits metamotivational versatility and can reverse easily between states may take advantage of this ability in his or her interaction with athletes. As Kerr (1993, pp. 413–414) stated:

Also, the sport psychologist who reverses in a 'healthy' manner, recognizable to the athlete, is more likely to encourage healthy reversal in the client athlete. Thus, a sport psychologist needs to understand his or her own reversal processes. For example, use of the technique of paradoxical intention (Frankl, 1973) requires the use of humor to enable the client athlete to develop a sense of detachment by laughing at, for example, anxiety. For this intervention to be successful it will require the sport psychologist to work, for much of the time, in the paratelic state (see also Bar-Eli, 1991).

For the sport psychologist who decides to utilise the reversal theory approach to counselling, a number of skills and abilities are necessary. First, he or she must be able to empathise with the client and understand the athlete's experience in terms of its nature, fabric and structure in terms of reversal theory. Second, he or she should be able to predict the probable structural impact of his or her own behaviour on the athlete during counselling. Third, this requires the sport psychologist to have the ability to act scientifically in the use of reversal theory's systematic structure, on which any choice of intervention technique and implementation is based. Fourth, he or she must have a sound knowledge of, and considerable practical skill in the implementation of a variety of intervention techniques. Fifth, the sport psychologist needs to have the personal interactive skills to be able to explain to the athlete the basic rationale of psychological reversals.

The first section of this chapter has focused on the counsellor rather than the athlete client. In particular, it has examined the underlying philosophy of the reversal theory approach to athlete problem assessment and intervention decision-making and has explained how the sport psychologist's own behaviour during counselling can affect the athlete in a positive way, helping to facilitate counselling sessions.

SPORT PSYCHOLOGIST: KNOW YOUR LIMITATIONS

All sport psychologists, including those basing their work on reversal theory, should be aware of their limitations. They may encounter some athlete problems that are beyond their expertise. If this occurs, then the sport psychologist should seek the assistance of a colleague who does have the necessary expertise. For example, unless a sport psychologist has had clinical training, some of the more complex behavioural or emotional problems, associated with inhibited reversals and inappropriate strategies described in the previous chapter, may go beyond the expertise of the psychologist concerned (e.g. Swoap and Murphy, 1995). Although it may be difficult (e.g. Kremer and Scully, 1994, p. 59), it is important for the sport psychologist to be able to recognise the difference between a temporary psychological performance problem and a full-blown clinical abnormality. The following case provides a good example of how a sport psychologist was able to provide athlete counselling on performance in tandem with another psychologist who was counselling the athlete for serious emotional problems.

LUCY: ATHLETE WITH COMPLICATIONS

Background

Lucy was a fit-looking, quite bubbly 19-year-old athlete who consulted a sport psychologist to try to improve her performance in the specialised role she occupied within her team. She had a series of five consultations just before her team competed in the World Championships. She had some prior knowledge of sport psychology through dealings with a team sport psychologist in general 'educational' seminars on improving performance in a group setting. However, she was critical of the fact that the psychologist had not seen the team play in competition or in practice and therefore could not know whether his ideas were having any effect on performance.

At the time of consultation, her situation was complicated by an ongoing alleged sexual abuse case involving a relationship between Lucy and her former coach, which was shortly due to be heard in court. Lucy was receiving separate counselling for the alleged abuse, meeting her counsellor weekly to discuss 'how things were' generally, and dealing with any repercussions of police findings as they came to hand. Lucy consulted the sport psychologist separately to help her deal with a performance problem. She had good support from her family and her current coach and assistant coach. Lucy's motivational style profile (Apter *et al.*, 1998) indicated that she was a highly telic–dominant athlete who also scored high on the effortfulness subscale (a tendency to pursue goals with energy and vigour and be undeterred by obstacles and frustrations).

Aware of a personal lack of competence in providing sexual abuse counselling, the sport psychologist contacted Lucy's sexual abuse counsellor before performance counselling began. The sport psychologist wanted to cooperate with the abuse counsellor and make sure that there was no conflict of interest involved. They agreed that the sport psychologist would concentrate on performance counselling, but would let Lucy talk about the sexual 'relationship' if she wished, merely acting as a sympathetic listener and offering no counselling advice on the matter.

Content

The sport psychologist had some basic knowledge of Lucy's sport, but was not familiar with the details of performance required at the elite level. In the first session, Lucy was asked to talk generally about her sport and the skills and abilities necessary to perform at a high level. This also helped to 'break the ice' and begin the process of developing empathy between psychologist and client. In addition, Lucy was asked to describe the intricacies of the different types of techniques that she used in playing and training. She showed the psychologist the different variations and described their function. She mentioned one variation she had had problems with in the past. She talked about her coaches and what they had told her about her performance and attitude. After about 45 minutes, as rapport began to become better established, Lucy began to talk about her previous coach and their sexual 'relationship'. Her eyes filled with tears. She wiped her eyes but continued with her story. Her emotions seemed close to the surface, but she made the effort to stay controlled and sounded very level-headed. Lucy described how on the last day of a three-week competition, the assistant coach and the other members of the team (all older than 18) went out for the night. Lucy, who was under-age and not interested in night-clubbing, stayed behind. The coach, who also remained behind, drank too much and forced himself on her. She was not a willing participant, she said. The 'relationship' continued on and off for several months, but Lucy said that she was still an unwilling participant. She eventually decided that she did not want to be around the coach any more, or have him around the other team members. She went to the police and reported it. (The description above is a shortened version of what Lucy said occurred.)

The sport psychologist listened sympathetically to Lucy, made a few neutral comments and checked that Lucy was satisfied with her participation in the abuse counselling sessions. Lucy indicated that she was. Subsequently, at the start of the second session, Lucy made it clear that she did not want the alleged abuse to be made the focus of the sport psychology counselling sessions. From this point on, and rather to the relief of the sport psychologist, who was very concerned about not making matters worse, the counselling sessions concentrated on Lucy's sport performance.

In the performance counselling sessions it became apparent that Lucy became 'pretty switched on' and really animated when she was talking about playing her sport. She said that she 'played brilliantly in competition' and enjoyed the opportunity that her sport provides to be aggressive and competitive against others. She also said that she loved the challenge of big matches, where her ability was put on the line in her specialist role within the team, where she had to make decisions about which of her technique variations to use in response to opposing players, and generally be responsible for controlling the game. Her goals were self-directed and seemed to be independent of external rewards; she wanted to see how far her talent would take her.

In contrast to her animation when talking about actually playing, Lucy talked about how boring her training sessions were because she was the only national team member in her area. This meant that she had to train alone or with a paid training partner. She said it was sometimes difficult to get a partner organised for days and times around her work, but boredom was the biggest off-putting factor. Getting more specific about the details of her training, Lucy said that her previous coach (the one involved in the court case) generated training regimes spontaneously, and training sessions varied in duration, at the coach's whim, from two to four hours. Lucy disliked this because she could not prepare herself for what was coming and could not pace herself over the sessions. She said she really enjoyed her current coach's training, which was based on about twelve different sheets which listed the order of practice. Lucy liked this because she could work through each sheet then put it on a pile of 'finished training pages' so she knew exactly how much more training she had to get through, and could experience a sense of satisfaction in 'ticking off' each completed sheet as it was done.

Coaches had told her that her technique was too slow and had attempted to use biomechanical analysis to try to correct the 'problem'. Lucy had four rivals for her position who were right-handers and whose techniques were faster. Lucy's technique was a little slower, but as a left-hander she had the advantage that she could add an extra dimension to her team's strategy. She admitted to having a specific problem with her technique on one particular variation, and felt negative about performing it. The coach taking the team to the world championships had told her that he was happy with her progress generally, although he had some concerns about her ability to perform under pressure. He had substituted her in a game where her technique went awry, resulting in some big scores for the opposing team. Lucy did not agree with that coach's assessment, and thought the games were not representative of her ability. She said she could generally put a poor technique out of her mind before the next one, and had enough faith to back her judgement. Lucy also explained how the coaches in her sport wanted everyone to be 'ra, ra' (cheering) for each other, even though she herself did not need the psyching up. She said she hated the falseness of this, but the coaches had directed that everyone must do it.

The sport psychologist noted that although Lucy was definitely not low on self-esteem, she could, perhaps, work on controlling negative thoughts which affected her confidence in certain circumstances, and that Lucy's independent thinking might be partly why she felt that her current coach and teammates thought she did not always fit in, and could be negative and sarcastic. Lucy tended to be a bit of a loner, and did not really care too much about what others thought of her.

Reversal theory interpretation

Lucy's statements about her likes and dislikes in the different types of training scenarios (planned, goal oriented and having prior knowledge of what is expected versus unplanned, spontaneous and not knowing what's coming next) point to her preferring to operate in the telic state during practice. Remember, for example, how she liked working progressively through each training sheet until the pile of 'finished training pages' was complete. When she was training without a planned, goal-oriented training programme, she found herself in the paratelic state, feeling bored.

However, when it comes to competition she may prefer to have the paratelic state operative. Her particular role within the team, where she was constantly under scrutiny and her ability was 'on the line', might be difficult for an athlete who was not in the paratelic state. Also, the fact that she loved the challenge of big matches would seem to support this view. Having the paratelic state operative during competition may also be related to superior performance (she 'plays brilliantly in competition'). Lucy would appear to prefer to be in the telic state for training and the paratelic state during matches.

While the nature of sport means that athletes are likely to be in the conformist state during much of the time when training and in competition, there is some evidence that Lucy is sometimes in the negativistic state. For example, her coach and teammates felt that she did not always fit in with her teammates and could be negative and sarcastic. Also, she did not like being directed by coaches to join in with the team cheering for each other, feeling that it was not helpful. As well as being negativistic, this reluctance to join in with team cheering and other signs also point to Lucy being predominantly in the autic and mastery states when performing. Her strong self-esteem assists her in her specialised role within the team, where her ability is frequently tested. Indeed, she could not fulfil her team role without a very strong element of autic–mastery metamotivation ('I enjoy the opportunity that my sport provides to be aggressive and competitive against others'), and being a bit of a loner may help her here.

Intervention strategy

In Lucy's case, the sport psychologist assessed her performance problem as being associated with inappropriate reversals (from the telic to the paratelic state) at training. Lucy did not appear to have a psychological problem at competition. The sport psychologist also assessed the predominantly operative autic–mastery state combination and the occasional negativistic behaviour as being important to Lucy's successful performance (within her specialised individual role in the team), and did not feel the need to intervene and try to change these aspects of performance metamotivation. Occasionally having the negativistic state operative was seen as an indication that Lucy was able to reverse in a 'healthy' manner, even when she was involved in the conformist-oriented team environment.

However, the sport psychologist did feel that it was important to make sure that Lucy was in the telic state during her practice sessions and for her to maximise the performance benefits while she was in this state. It was thought that an intervention making use of goal-setting techniques, as an extension to the telic-oriented progressive practice that she preferred, could achieve this. The aim was to improve the quality of the different variations of her technique, particularly the one that she had had trouble with in the past. The psychologist and Lucy agreed that she should try to quantify the quality of each technique, focusing on how well she felt the technique was executed and whether or not it hit the expected target area. A scoring format was worked out which would let Lucy see whether she had improved, both over the duration of an individual training session and over the weeks of training.

In addition, some key words were generated to associate with each of the technique variations which could be used to assist Lucy in remembering the specific hand–arm arrangement that would lead to more accurate execution of each variation. Lucy had also been unaware that how she felt about the variation that she had been having difficulty with, might actually affect how she performed it (e.g. stance, muscle tension, effort). She agreed to try extra hard to use the particular key word for this variation, with the addendum 'be positive' when executing it. The latter was to help control negative thoughts which sometimes affected Lucy's confidence about executing this particular variation.

For the forthcoming world championships, the sport psychologist was keen that Lucy should use these key words, but not focus too much on evaluating the execution of her technique during the game. Evaluating her technique might induce the telic state. It was important that Lucy continued to have her performance-enhancing paratelic state operative during play. Therefore, time was also spent discussing aspects of the world championships environment, such as crowd effects and delays in play, and the effect these might have on her frame of mind. The crowd was likely to be larger and noisier than Lucy was used to, but it was pointed out that she could use this to her advantage by enjoying it in the paratelic state, rather than being intimidated by it and allowing it to affect her mental state. Lucy knew what to do to lift herself for the big occasion, but they also discussed situations where play might be delayed (for example, owing to rain) and how Lucy could regain her preferred high levels of arousal when play resumed.

The counselling climate

The unresolved court case cast a serious, telic shadow over most aspects of Lucy's life at the time she came for performance counselling. In addition, she was highly telic dominant. Therefore, it seemed likely that the adoption of a very serious approach to Lucy's problems would not be helpful. A paratelic feel to the counselling sessions might prove to be useful, as this might induce the paratelic state in Lucy and perhaps make her more receptive to new ideas. However, even when she did have the paratelic state operative, she was liable to reverse back to the telic state if and when the sexual abuse issue arose during the performance counselling.

Realising the sensitive nature of the counselling sessions, the psychologist decided to let Lucy take the lead and pick up cues from her as she went along. As it turned out, there were fairly frequent reversals in the sessions, with plenty of light-hearted moments and laughter on some occasions, and tears streaming down Lucy's face on others. The sexual abuse issue came up in the first session, but was much less of a problem in the later sessions.

The suggestions made by the psychologist about quantifying performance and using key words were actually telic in orientation when put into practice, but in counselling they appealed to Lucy (in the paratelic state) as new and interesting ways of dealing with her problem. It was then up to Lucy to take the ideas from the counselling room to the playing arena and put them into practice as part of her telic-oriented training.

Outcome

The counselling work helped Lucy improve the accuracy and consistency of her techniques, and she reported that the coach, who had previously been concerned about her performance, was now satisfied about the style and speed of her variations on technique. By the time she was ready to leave for the world championships,

Lucy had also begun to feel really settled and was looking forward to the tournament (probably the sexual abuse counselling played a role in this as well). At the championships she performed outstandingly well, eclipsing her right-handed rivals. Lucy was told by the coach that her ranking in the team had changed from third to first choice because of her effective play under pressure.

She was looking forward to playing the following season, just wanting to put the sexual abuse case behind her, and to concentrate totally on improving her sport performance.

Postscript

Lucy's former coach was charged with and pleaded guilty to five counts of having consensual sex with a minor under his care, supervision or authority. He received a three-year suspended sentence and was banned from taking part in his sport for ten years.

CLOSING COMMENTS

The latter part of this final chapter emphasised that sport psychologists need to be aware of any personal limitation to their areas of competence. This means that on some occasions, athletes who have sought out counselling for particular problems should be referred to colleagues. Needless to say, sport psychologists who have the athlete's psychological health and welfare foremost in their minds will do this willingly. In the case of Lucy, a useful working relationship was arrived at between sport psychologist and sexual abuse counsellor which was of benefit to Lucy. However, while it was important to make this point, it brings the discussion into the area of ethics in sport psychology practice, and any further discussion would go well beyond the boundaries of this book.

The main purpose of this chapter was to examine the role of the sport psychologist and show how he or she could take advantage of reversal theory, both prior to and during counselling sessions with athletes. It should be apparent that the benefit of reversal theory is not to be found in some new technique, perhaps known as 'reversal therapy' (Apter, 1989, p. 154). Rather, as has been emphasised throughout this book, reversal theory can provide a systematic conceptual framework for carrying out eclectic athlete counselling. This framework can guide the sport psychologist through an understanding and evaluation of the nature of each individual athlete's problem(s), assist with decisions about the goals of counselling, and provide a sound theoretical foundation on which the psychologist can base selection from a range of techniques and therapeutic interventions (Apter, 1989; Kerr, 1993). As Apter (1989, p. 150) pointed out:

> What reversal theory does is not to identify new syndromes which no one had suspected existed. What it does is to take a wide variety of psychological

problems and show how they fit into a structure which had not previously been discerned, disclosing new patterns and relationships between them in the process.

The reversal theory approach to athlete counselling can be seen as a model of therapeutic integration, a framework for eclectic practice in sport psychology (Murgatroyd, 1987c).

SUGGESTED FURTHER READING

Lafreniere, K. D., Ledgerwood, D. M. and Murgatroyd, S. J. (2001) 'Psychopathology, therapy and counselling', in M. J. Apter (ed.) *Motivational Lifestyles in Everyday Life: A Guide to Reversal Theory*, Washington, DC: American Psychological Association.
Apter, M. J. (1989) *Reversal Theory: Motivation, Emotion and Personality*, London: Routledge.
Kerr, J. H. (1993) 'An eclectic approach to psychological interventions in sport: reversal theory', *The Sport Psychologist* 7: 400–418.

FOR DISCUSSION

1   Construct your own imaginary case of an athlete who comes to you, as a sport psychologist, for performance counselling. Using reversal theory's eclectic approach to athlete counselling, describe your client's background, the main content of any counselling sessions and a reversal theory interpretation of the content. In addition, justify your choice of intervention strategy and its goals, explaining the counselling climate you would attempt to produce and the desired outcome of your counselling.

2   Think about the case of Lucy. Are there other circumstances which might arise in athlete counselling which would require a sport psychologist to refer an athlete client to another psychologist?

FINAL STATEMENT

Whether you are a practising sport psychologist, an athlete, an academic, a student or a lay person, it is hoped that as you reach the end of this book, the explanations and arguments included here have been sufficient to convince you of the value of reversal theory in athlete counselling. Already a number of athletes, some recorded as case material in this book, have benefited from reversal theory's eclectic athlete counselling and gone forward to perform successfully. Whether or not you take on board the reversal theory approach in your work is, of course, a matter of personal choice, but perhaps the last word should be left to Lafreniere *et al.* (2001):

> A reversal theory approach can guide therapists to facilitate in their clients the flexibility and knowledge to achieve optimal satisfaction and effectiveness in all the complexities of their metamotivational experience. To put it at its simplest, they can help clients to be 'in the right state at the right time in the right way'.

Appendix

The role of response satiation in overtraining and burnout in sports

Oscar Randall Braman

The basic process by which responses become satiated has been known for the past fifty years, and satiation as a concept can be found as an essential element in almost all theories of behaviour. Psychologists may debate the details, or offer differing terminology and theoretical interpretations for why responses become satiated, but when all of that is set aside, the universally accepted explanation is that responses become satiated from being practised. Furthermore, satiation is always specific to the response which produced it, and interferes with that response but does not interfere with other responses. The assumption is that each time a response is made, a reluctance to repeat that response builds up, and when the response is rested, this reluctance gradually diminishes. With continued repetition of a response, the reluctance can build up to the point that the response no longer occurs. The inability to make a particular response as a result of having just made that response a critical number of times is what is meant when it is said that the response is 'satiated'. A response which is satiated, therefore, does not occur. Rewarded responses may take more repetitions before they succumb to satiation, but even rewarded responses will eventually stop being made if they are repeated enough times. When as a result of satiation a response stops being made, the satiation itself thus imposes a rest, allowing the satiation associated with that particular response to begin to gradually subside. When enough time has passed for the satiation to diminish significantly, the response will begin occurring again at a rate almost equal to the response rate before satiation set in. The reappearance of a previously satiated response in this way is called 'spontaneous recovery'.

Coaches and athletes in order to be successful seek procedures that maximise the beneficial effects and minimise the harmful effects of training. They have to learn how to pace the rate and vigour of practice in such a way as to reach 'peak' performance at the right time, a goal which, among other things, is a matter of balancing the benefits of practice against losses due to satiation, physical fatigue and other negative effects. A powerful aid in this endeavour is the relatively new discipline of sport psychology. Sport psychologists apply the science of psychology to any and all aspects of sport, and in recent years have turned their attention to overtraining and its relationship to burnout (e.g. Coakley, 1992; Hollander *et al.*, 1995; McCann, 1995; Smith, 1986), subject-matter to which the research and theories concerning response satiation would seem to be especially relevant.

Satiation as a concept, by whatever name it is identified, has proven of value in the prediction, control and understanding of behaviour in a wide variety of circumstances. In order to understand its role in behaviour theory in general, and in particular its role in reversal theory (Apter, 1982), a brief history of the theoretical development of this concept is offered. In doing so, there is the dual purpose of helping those who are involved in sport better understand satiation, and better understand reversal theory. Such understanding may help coaches and athletes find not only improved procedures for avoiding burnout and the harmful effects of overtraining, but may also help them find ways in which burnout and overtraining, under proper conditions, can prove beneficial.

RESPONSE-SPECIFIC SATIATION VERSUS FATIGUE

Satiation is important in understanding an essential but often neglected difference between living organisms and machines. Machines in reasonably good condition can repeat the same action endlessly, while healthy living organisms must from time to time change what they are doing. Living organisms are typically reluctant to repeat endlessly so-called 'voluntary' actions, regardless of how rewarding the actions may be. Under any circumstances, and with any living organism, there is always a limit to how many times a response will be repeated, and though the limiting factor is often considered to be physical fatigue, living organisms typically reach the limit of their tolerance for repeating the same response much sooner than they reach the limits of their physical endurance. Humans and animals get *tired of* doing something long before they get *tired*. This suggests that when a response is made, though a certain amount of physical fatigue may be generated, even more significant is that each time it is made it becomes a little more 'satiated'; that is, a little more of some sort of psychological 'inhibition' associated with that particular response builds up. Unlike fatigue, satiation of a specific response curtails the tendency to repeat that response, but does not affect the tendency to make other responses. Thus an organism experiencing large amounts of response-specific satiation is reluctant to make some particular response, while an organism experiencing large amounts of physical fatigue is reluctant to do anything.

SECHENOV'S THEORY OF INHIBITION

Response-specific inhibition of so-called 'voluntary' responses was postulated in 1863 by I. M. Sechenov, who offered this concept in an explanation for why 'thinking' in human adults does not ordinarily involve the kind of overt motor activities which children typically display when occupied with mental tasks. In his *Reflexes of the Brain*, Sechenov (1863/1965) suggests that the talking and gesturing that children engage in when carrying out mental tasks become over the years increasingly associated with inhibition, and are thus gradually eliminated. The result of this is that for adults, 'thinking' occurs with little or no talking or gesturing. That Sechenov does not consider that 'thinking' might itself produce inhibition and thus be eliminated along with the motor activity may reflect a tacit assumption on his part that since 'thinking' takes so little work, it would produce very little inhibition in comparison with motor activities. According to Sechenov, therefore, because so little work is required, even after extensive repetition 'thinking' would continue to occur, while the motor activities associated with it, which require much greater work, would be eliminated. The notion that the more work responses take, the more inhibition they produce, and thus when practised the quicker and more certain they will be weakened or eliminated, is often implicitly, and sometimes explicitly, assumed by those who subscribe to the concept of response-specific inhibition.

In discussing how humans habituate to emotions, Sechenov recognised that stimuli repeatedly presented to a subject produce a reluctance to respond even when the stimuli are pleasurable:

> Man is so constructed that a frequently repeated impression, no matter how pleasant, begins to pall him; many people even go farther and say that our nerves are so constructed that they are fatigued by a pleasant impression, if it is frequently repeated.
>
> (Sechenov, 1863/1965, p. 92)

In the same passage, he says that a pleasure lost because it has been repeated too much may be regained after a period of abstention from it. From these remarks it would seem that Sechenov assumed that (1) as far as inhibition is concerned, it does not matter whether a response leads to pleasant consequences or not; a response produces inhibition as readily when it is rewarded as it does when it occurs without reward; and (2) if a response is not made for a period of time, the inhibition associated with it may dissipate and the response regain its previous strength. These are certainly two important aspects of the concept of inhibition, but ones that have proven over the years to be complex and controversial. Sechenov's 'inhibition' is, of course, the earliest term used to denote 'satiation'.

PAVLOV'S THEORY OF INHIBITION

Inhibition is also central in the theory of conditioning proposed by I. P. Pavlov (1926/1960). His basic experimental design is well known: a bell is rung and a dog is given food, and this process is repeated until the dog begins to salivate as soon as the bell is rung and before the food is given. The food, according to Pavlov, is the reinforcement which conditions the dog to salivate to the bell. Many American psychologists are prone to use the term 'reinforcement' to simply mean 'reward', and to argue that in Pavlov's experiments, the dog *learns* to salivate to the bell because the food makes it rewarding to do so. After the dog has been conditioned to salivate (has learned to salivate) to the bell, if the bell is then rung repeatedly with no food being given, the dog will gradually cease to salivate to the bell. To no longer salivate to the bell because no food is given is called 'experimental extinction'.

According to Pavlov, there are several types of inhibition. 'Internal inhibition' is the type produced when responses are made. Experimental extinction is totally due to the build-up of this type of inhibition. He rejected, however, the notion that rewarded responses produce inhibition. He claimed that only non-reinforced (non-rewarded) responses produce inhibition, a conclusion which seems perhaps to be intuitively valid, but which contradicts Sechenov's assumption, and which is contradicted in turn by extensive research in subsequent years.

Pavlov found that experimental extinction is not a permanent phenomenon. In every case where a conditioned response has undergone experimental extinction, the extinct response 'invariably becomes spontaneously restored in a longer or shorter time' (Pavlov, 1926/1960, p. 67). The transitory nature of experimental extinction establishes that the inhibition producing the extinction, which in turn was produced by responding, dissipates with time. This finding, with some qualifications, has been amply confirmed by subsequent research.

The effects of the amount of work responses take were not given consideration in Pavlov's research, nor did he study the so-called 'voluntary' responses which were Sechenov's main interest. Pavlov devoted himself almost exclusively to the seemingly almost effortless salivation reflex, hardly a response the study of which one would expect would clarify such issues as the relationship between over-training and burnout in sports.

But Pavlov launched a scientific method for studying behaviour, provided a language for describing results, and discovered many basic psychological phenomena. He managed to objectively test some of Sechenov's ideas which had been put forward originally in rather vague, subjective ways. Although Pavlov's theoretical and experimental research on inhibition may be called into question today, he must be credited, more than anyone else, for bringing attention to the subject of response-produced inhibition, and in so doing starting us on an understanding of the modern concept of satiation.

HULL'S THEORY OF INHIBITION

It is in its theoretical development by Clark Hull (1943) that inhibition gains its usefulness in understanding the relationship between overtraining and burnout. Sechenov had implied that in some cases the effects of response-produced inhibition might be relatively permanent, while Pavlov claimed that they were always extremely transient. Both failed to specify the determinants for producing relatively permanent inhibition, and neither Sechenov nor Pavlov attempted to identify all the specific conditions under which inhibition dissipates. Furthermore, they did not concern themselves with the relationship between the amount of work a response takes and the amount of inhibition it produces, and they disagreed on whether responses produce inhibition when rewarded. Hull worked through these contradictions, lapses and conflicting assumptions, finally producing a single systematic theory of inhibition. Furthermore, his theory relates inhibition to 'instrumental' behaviour, a term used by behaviourists to denote what Sechenov would have called 'voluntary'. Thus Hull's theory elucidates the relationship between inhibition and the behaviour which most interested Sechenov, which of course is the type of behaviour of most interest to coaches and athletes.

Many pioneer American psychologists before Hull had observed that behaviour satiates, that is, that living organisms are reluctant to make the same response repeatedly (e.g. Young, 1936, p. 249). They had observed the very same behavioural phenomenon which Sechenov and Pavlov attributed to the effects of response-produced inhibition, but showed an antipathy towards the term 'inhibition'. They attributed this phenomenon to 'mental fatigue' (Thorndike, 1914/1949), 'negative adaptation' (Dennis and Sollenberger, 1934; Woodworth, 1921), 'habituation' (Dodge, 1923), or other comparable constructs. The term 'inhibition' was not widely used by American psychologists until Hull, in the 1930s and 1940s, began to precisely delineate what Sechenov and Pavlov had perhaps rather inconsistently included under the rubric of 'inhibition'.

Reactive inhibition

A product of extensive investigation of experimental extinction and spontaneous recovery, Hull's 'Postulate 8' states that when a response occurs, whether rewarded or not, it produces 'reactive inhibition'. Reactive inhibition is defined as a type of hypothetical resistance which functions to decrease the probability that a particular response will be repeated. The more work a response takes, and the more often it is made, the more of this inhibition will be produced. When the response is not being made, the reactive inhibition associated with it gradually dissipates. Resting from the response and letting reactive inhibition dissipate is rewarding to the organism (Hull, 1943, p. 300).

The most important assumption of Hull's theory is that rewarded responses tend to become learned, and the more often responses are rewarded and the greater the rewards each time they occur, the stronger is the learning (Postulate 4, p. 178). Thus when an animal or human is engaged in rewarding activities, because the strength of the learned tendencies is increasing, the effects of reactive inhibition may not at first become apparent. It is not known to what extent reactive inhibition can build up, but there are always limits to how strong learned tendencies can become. When responses continue to be made beyond the limits of learning, no matter how rewarding they may be, the continued production of reactive inhibition will cause the responses to weaken, become disrupted and eventually stop all together; that is, the responses will eventually satiate. Like learning, motivation may temporarily conceal the effects of reactive inhibition (Postulate 7, p. 253). But motivation also has limits, and furthermore, motivation is difficult to maintain, thus making certain that regardless of the degree of motivation, if behaviour continues without rest or change, satiation will occur.

Despite rewards for the behaviour and high levels of motivation, if the behaviour continues unabated, sooner or later reactive inhibition will take its toll. Support for this assertion can be found in such research as that on 'reminiscence', where rests or changes in behaviour during practice produce immediate improved performance (Ballard, 1913; Ward, 1937); on the 'spacing effect' in learning, where practice interrupted with rest periods produces much better performance than when the practice is continuous (Dempster, 1988; Kientzle, 1946); on the 'involuntary rest pause', where if no rests are allowed, performance simply ceases periodically (Bills, 1931); and that on 'spontaneous alternation behavior', where animals and humans when possible alternate the way they carry out a task (Richman, 1989; Zeaman and House, 1951). Although in this kind of research the differences between the effects of reactive inhibition and those of physical fatigue are usually obvious, it must be noted that confusion is possible; it must be remembered that reactive inhibition is a reluctance affecting the specific response which has just been made, while physical fatigue manifests itself as a generalised reluctance affecting all responses.

Conditioned inhibition

According to Hull, reactive inhibition is temporary, and dissipates with rest. Thus the transient and evanescent qualities which Pavlov claimed characterised all response-produced inhibition, Hull attributes to reactive inhibition. The relatively permanent type of inhibition produced when a response is repeated, which Sechenov emphasised, Hull calls 'conditioned inhibition'. Conditioned inhibition is not directly the result of satiation, but is rather learning to avoid making the satiated response; that is, learning to do something else. One set of antecedents which lead to the conditioned inhibition of a response is 'extinction training'. Extinction training is making the response repeatedly under conditions of no reward. It is important to note that motivation must be present during extinction training: rewards are absent but motivation is present, a crucial distinction. If motivation were not present during extinction training, there would be no activation of the response, and thus no way the response could occur and undergo conditions of no reward. When extinction training is continued long enough for reactive inhibition to build up sufficiently for satiation to occur – that is, for the response to cease – the resulting rest and dissipation of inhibition reinforces (rewards) the act of not responding. Thus each time extinction training is carried out, two things happen: first, reactive inhibition increases to the point that, despite the motivation present, the response ceases; and second, when the response ceases, the rewarding consequences of not responding increase the tendency to not respond in that situation in the future. Learning to not respond in a particular situation defines what is meant by conditioned inhibition. Conditioned inhibition does not dissipate, being simply the acquisition of new incompatible behaviour in place of the previously repeated response.

Because of conditioned inhibition, a response which has undergone extinction never recovers completely. When extinction training eliminates a response, the response spontaneously recovers, though not completely, as Pavlov claimed, but only to the extent to which its elimination is due to *reactive* inhibition. Each time a response undergoes extinction it is easier to eliminate, and the less it spontaneously recovers; this is because with each extinction, conditioned inhibition increases, and less reactive inhibition is needed to cause the response to become satiated. Since reactive inhibition dissipates with rest, the less reactive inhibition involved, the less will be the spontaneous recovery. With each period of non-reward, the extinction of the response is due more to conditioned inhibition and less to reactive inhibition, and though it may take several periods of non-reward, eventually the elimination of the response becomes totally the result of having learned not to make the response in that situation. When this happens, the extinction of the response is relatively permanent, and spontaneous recovery will no longer take place.

Involuntary rest pauses

The basic events described above are not unique to extinction training. Under all conditions of continuous practice, especially when the responses involved entail large amounts of work, reactive inhibition builds up, interfering with performance. This effect of continuous practice is at first often hidden, especially when rewards are great and motivation is high. The presence of rewards and motivation, however, in no way alters the build-up of reactive inhibition. In cases of overtraining, even rewarded behaviour with maximum motivation will eventually satiate. Reactive inhibition can increase until it cancels out the effects of the rewards and the motivation. When this happens, the responses stop for a period long enough to allow just enough of the reactive inhibition to dissipate for the responses to start again. When they start again, if no rest is allowed, they soon build up more reactive inhibition, resulting in another stoppage. These response stoppages, called 'involuntary rest pauses' (Bills, 1931), do not, however, occur in isolation but are associated with brief lapses of attention, mistakes, missed timings, and other signs of temporarily deteriorating performance.

When a response is repeated continuously for long periods, the involuntary rest pauses which result make for the development of conditioned inhibition. The rest and dissipation of reactive inhibition which take place during the rest pause reward the organism for not making the response in the situation. In this way, a tendency to not make the response is learned (conditioned inhibition), and this learned tendency to not make the response, or to do something else, is relatively permanent and functions to reduce more or less permanently the amount of spontaneous recovery for that response. Thus as in extinction training, when the response is temporarily eliminated and after a rest spontaneously recovers, it always falls short of complete recovery.

In the case of overtraining, after involuntary rest pauses have begun to occur, performance is at first interfered with only by fragmentary tendencies towards doing nothing, or towards doing something else; that is, sluggishness and intermittent lapses of attention which give rise to mistakes, missed timings, staleness, etc. If an adequate rest period is introduced, the athlete may seem to recover, but if overtraining is repeated, relatively permanent negative effects will accumulate. Despite the fact that the behaviour may be rewarding, and despite the fact that optimal motivation may be present, with repeated periods of overtraining, the fragmentary tendencies to do nothing will eventually coalesce into strong and relatively permanent tendencies to completely terminate the behaviour being practised. That is, repeated periods of overtraining will eventually lead to what is perhaps most appropriately termed 'burnout'.

WHAT IS BURNOUT?

People and animals sooner or later abandon behaviour they find unrewarding. When behaviour ceases because of non-reward, it is said to be extinguished or to have become extinct. Sometimes the apathy resulting from failing to achieve rewards in a given situation is called 'conditioned helplessness'. Although there may be those who consider the elimination of behaviour due to non-reward, and the conditioned helplessness which sometimes follows, to be 'burnout', these commonly recognised effects of non-reward hardly warrant so dramatic a term. It is certainly not unusual for persons who have engaged in particular jobs or activities for several months or years to finally discover that they are not enjoying them, and it is not surprising or remarkable that under such circumstance they seek other ways to spend their time. But abandoning behaviour because of non-reward is much less complex than abandoning it because of burnout. Burnout is a much more intense, stressful and paradoxical phenomenon.

Working on chain gangs, in sweat shops, in death camps, and in other manner of forced labour certainly gives rise to satiation, is almost totally devoid of reward, and any tendencies to continue in this kind of work certainly extinguish, producing conditioned helplessness. However, we do not need the concept of burnout to explain the elimination of tendencies to continue to behave under these conditions. These are simply extreme examples of situations where behaviour is abandoned because it is generally unpleasant.

By contrast, individuals facing possible burnout do not find what they are doing unpleasant. They are not only highly motivated, but find their activities rewarding – more often than not, exceedingly so. Burnout occurs because the individuals' high motivation and the rewards they obtain encourage them to overwork, to fail to take time off, fail to rest, and fail to switch to other behaviours periodically.

As a way of relating what has been said here with reversal theory (Apter, 1982), burnout could be postulated as being due to the satiation of sets of generalised goal-directed behaviours organised around the 'telic–conformity state'. To be 'telic' means to be goal directed, and to be 'conforming' means to be guided by other people's requirements. As satiation of the behavioural sets associated with the telic–conformist state builds up, there begin to occur involuntary reversals to a purposeless, negativistic state (reversals not unlike the 'involuntary rest pauses' which occur as a result of satiation in all types of work). For people who take their careers seriously, who 'love' their jobs and gain gratification in living up to the expectations of others – namely, those who are most often in the telic–conformist state – when such people find themselves inexplicably and involuntarily shifting to aimless, negativistic behaviour, it is to them extremely disturbing and stressful.

As burnout develops, the individuals discover much to their chagrin that they can no longer reliably behave in ways which previously gained them crucial rewards. Their confidence and self-esteem suffer, and often all they want to do is to get totally away from the situation. Burnout, which is the product of rewarded behaviour carried to extreme, therefore ends by taking the rewards out of the situation, ultimately causing them to abandon what they are doing. Burnout can lead to the termination of the careers of successful schoolteachers, police officers, nurses, physicians, emergency medical workers, coaches, and others who constantly take on social responsibilities. The victims of burnout tend to be people whom others admire, depend on, and to whom one can turn in times of need. When burnout happens to athletes, more often than not it is to the best, most motivated and serious that it happens.

Sean McCann, a member of the United States Olympic Committee, describes just such an athlete:

The case of Cindy

Cindy is an elite bicycle racer in her late teens. She quickly rose in earlier years to elite status, showing talent and, even more markedly, an amazing work ethic and an ability to train harder than anyone else. Cindy felt more confident when she knew that she had ridden more miles and had done more high-intensity training than her competitors. Now at the senior elite level, she has found that her improvement has slowed considerably. . . . Unsatisfied with her rate of progress . . . she began extra evening training rides without her coach's knowledge. . . . She and her coaches began noticing significant negative changes in her performance. . . . Cindy appeared sluggish and slow to respond to attacks in training rides. In sprint and interval sessions, Cindy was losing ground to riders she had earlier beaten easily. She began to complain of chronic knee pain and developed a cough that wouldn't go away. Perhaps even more disturbing to the coaches were changes in Cindy's personality. Always the first to arrive at training sessions, she often arrived late and appeared sleepy.

Previously a positive and exuberant athlete, Cindy began to complain about minor equipment problems and other team members. As the training season progressed, Cindy began expressing doubts about her ability and on two occasions quit training sessions in tears. After she missed an important race due to oversleeping and missing a ride, her coaches called a conference to discuss Cindy's attitude and to determine if she belonged in the elite cycling program.

(McCann, 1995, pp. 347–348)

From what is known concerning the determinants and effects of satiation, sport would be particularly vulnerable to burnout. Sport is, for the participants, demanding but highly rewarding. Most sport behaviour satiates rapidly because of the large expenditure of energy involved, and because the range of responses practised are usually circumscribed. Repeating, over and over, precise and energetic sets of movements, as one does in training for most sports, makes satiation almost a certainty. The dedicated, highly motivated athlete, therefore, always faces the risk of training too much.

But training too much is sometimes beneficial. When athletes develop faulty ways of behaving which are preventing them from performing at their best, and if ordinary instruction and coaching fail to overcome the problem, then 'burning out' the impeding behaviour may work. Most coaches have learned how to use overtraining for specific purposes such as this, and it is hoped that with better understanding of response satiation this skill can be enhanced and expanded.

BURNOUT IN A GROUP OF MOTIVATED LABORATORY RATS

Hans Eysenck describes how overtraining, even in laboratory rats, can lead to burnout. The following account shows that with repeated periods of overtraining, the build-up and dissipation of reactive inhibition can lead to the development of conditioned inhibition and the relatively permanent termination of the practised behaviour:

In one of our experiments rats that had been deprived of water for 23 hours were taught to run down an alleyway for a few drops of water. The run was repeated 30 times in succession, leaving the rats still somewhat short of complete satisfaction. They were then removed to a neutral cage for an hour and were finally returned to their own cages, where unlimited food and water were available. This regime was repeated day after day on the assumption that the gradual growth of conditioned inhibition would finally lead to a complete cessation of alleyway-running in spite of the strong thirst drive under which the rats were working. It was a close call as to whether conditioned inhibition would develop earlier in the rat than in the experimenter, but finally all the rats did in fact perform as predicted, remaining in their starting boxes and refusing to run in spite of having been without water for 23 hours.

(Eysenck, 1963, p. 4)

BEYOND BURNOUT

In this appendix, the terms 'response satiation', 'response-produced inhibition' and 'reactive inhibition' have been considered equivalent. The fact is that the terminology for discussing response satiation varies from one psychologist to another, and from one epoch to another. Diversity of terms hinders researchers from recognising that they may be dealing with a single phenomenon. If the diverse terminology is transcended, the phenomenon of response satiation appears to have important implications over wide areas of human and animal behaviour. The lines of research, however, which have been begun need to be followed up. Only with such follow-up research can the real value of this concept be fully realised.

Effects of response satiation have been observed in the behaviour of such simple organisms as paramecia (Lepley and Rice, 1952) and planarians (Best, 1963). The claim has been made that schizophrenics dissipate reactive inhibition more slowly than do persons in the general population (Eysenck, 1961). Infants who build up reactive inhibition more rapidly – that is, those that 'habituate' more rapidly – are said to be more intelligent (Cohen, 1976). Response satiation seems to be the only satisfactory explanation for the so-called 'Law of Least Effort', namely, the long-observed fact that as people and animals practise a task, superfluous and unnecessary responses, especially those requiring greater effort, gradually drop out (Hull, 1943, pp. 293–295). And the adage that 'creativity is more a matter of perspiration than inspiration' can be understood if one recognises that discovering totally new ways of doing things is more likely when old and ordinary ways have, owing to long hours of fruitless and effortful repetition, become satiated (Barron, 1969).

RESPONSE SATIATION IN HABIT BREAKING AND BEHAVIOUR MODIFICATION

E. R. Guthrie (1935) introduced the term 'exhaustion method' to denote those techniques for breaking bad habits which entail massive practice of the undesirable behaviour. Hans Eysenck, following his description above of how massive practice eliminated alleyway-running in laboratory rats, states:

We have since applied this same principle to the elimination of tics and other automatic neurotic habits in human patients by making them repeat the unwanted movements over and over again under conditions of massed practice. In many cases the neurotic habit is extinguished completely and in others its intensity is much reduced.

(Eysenck, 1963, p. 4)

Among the extremely numerous therapeutic techniques utilising the potency of response satiation for their effectiveness are 'desensitisation' (Wolpe, 1958), 'cognitive rehearsal' (Foxman, 1972), 'implosive therapy' (Stumpfl and Levis, 1967) and even 'paradoxical intention' (Frankl, 1960). One of the pioneers in the use of the exhaustion method was Knight Dunlap, using this technique for the treatment of stammering. The person who stammers should:

> . . . be ready to practice stammering under the psychologist's direction, eagerly and enthusiastically. . . . He should be led to engage in it without inhibition, doubt or qualms. This is especially important. The periods of practice will vary from case to case. In some cases half an hour a day will be adequate . . . have the patient practice stammering a phrase until he stammers it well, and then immediately [have him] speak it correctly. If he succeeds on first trial, he may repeat it once or twice. If he fails, he should be stopped at the first appearance of stammering, and stammering practice should be immediately renewed. Avoid, above all, during the practice period, having the patient trying to speak correctly and failing.
>
> (Dunlap, 1932/1972, pp. 204–205)

IMPLICATIONS FOR REVERSAL THEORY

A basic principle of reversal theory (Apter, 1982, p. 41) is that metamotivational states satiate, and when they do, reversals into the opposite states occur. In terms of what is known concerning the determinants of satiation, although clearly not a formal assumption of reversal theory, it would seem that a metamotivational state would be more likely to satiate when the individual in that state is engaged in greater amounts of highly repetitive, effortful activity. Thus athletes in the paratelic–negativistic state, who, as a result of being in that state, find enjoyment in aimlessly and playfully rebelling against whatever anyone else is trying to get them to do, do not seem likely to engage for very long in repetitious, effortful activity. Athletes in the telic–conformist state, on the other hand, are more likely to diligently practise effortful, precise behaviours for long periods of time. This does not mean that the paratelic and negativistic states do not satiate, only that athletes in these states are much less likely to satiate than those in the telic and conformist states. It would seem, therefore, that for athletes in the telic–conformist state who are tempted to overtrain, reversing to the paratelic–negativistic state is an eventuality which is always imminent.

Being in a playful paratelic state is generally pleasant; but would this be true for serious, conscientious, telic-dominant athletes who are gearing up for competitive sport? Would such individuals enjoy finding themselves shifting inexplicably into a playful, paratelic state? If, in addition to being telic dominant, the athletes are conformist dominant, as the serious, conscientious athlete may very likely be, reversing to the negativistic state, where they find themselves inexplicably feeling rebellious against coaches and officials, would hardly be pleasant to them. Thus because of involuntary reversals to the opposite state which occur with over-training, telic–conformist-dominant athletes who repeatedly overtrain are very likely to find their sport activities more and more stressful and punishing. As a result, avoiding the sport becomes rewarding (creating conditioned inhibition), and thus, like the laboratory rats in Eysenck's experiment, the athletes learn to no longer participate in the sport, and more or less permanently give it up; that is, they burn out.

At this point it is not clear how any but telic–conformity-dominant individuals locked into the telic–conformity state could be at risk for burnout, but it would be premature to exclude other possibilities. The hypothesis presented here is that burnout is likely to occur to athletes who repeatedly overtrain because they are highly motivated and find the training highly rewarding, who are more or less 'trapped' or 'stuck' in the telic–conformity state, and who find the paratelic and the negativistic states unsettling and unpleasant. One possible variation of this pattern might be athletes who overtrain in response to pressuring parents who, by subtle threats of loss of love, keep them in a telic–conformist state until reversals to the telic–self-negativistic state called 'oppositionalism' involuntarily occur (Braman, 1982/1999, 1988). In general, athletes who can reverse easily and appropriately, though they may frequently overtrain, are not likely to burn out. Athletes who are locked in the telic–conformist state, and who because of this risk burning out, are apparently the antithesis of the addict and hooligan, on and off the playing field, who find pleasure only in the paratelic state (Brown, 1991; Kerr, 1994).

IMPLICATIONS FOR COACHES AND ATHLETES

Although generally true, the adage that 'practice makes perfect', if believed in too rigidly, is potentially harmful, especially if the further notion is rigidly accepted that 'the more practice the better'. Most coaches and athletes, however, know that time spent away from training is as crucial to success as time spent in training. This analysis, in clarifying the differences between fatigue and satiation, expands on why frequent changes in behaviour are necessary, and helps in the identification of those conditions under which rest and practice should take place. The research on satiation summarised here makes more understandable what has been reported by sport psychologists, namely, that athletes who repeatedly overtrain may manifest such early symptoms of potential burnout as distractibility, apathy, depression, diminished concentration, loss of self-esteem, fear of competition, and intimations of giving up (Hollander et al., 1995). Most important is the recognition that it is the most cooperative and diligent athletes, the ones who consider themselves, and are considered by their coaches, to be the least disruptive, who are most likely to overtrain and are at greatest risk for burnout. It should be noted that coaches also experience burnout (Smith, 1986, p. 39), and it may be that the personal qualities which put coaches at risk for burnout are the same as those which put athletes at risk.

In certain circumstances, overtraining may be beneficial. Although the effects of unchecked overtraining can take as much as three months for full recovery (Hollander *et al.*, 1995), judiciously used with appropriate rest periods, techniques incorporating excessive training can result in peak physical state at competition (McCann, 1995). Using excessive training, or, as it is called in this context, 'overload training' or 'overwork', for this purpose is undoubtedly an undertaking that only the best and most experienced coaches should attempt.

There are, however, techniques using overtraining for beneficial purposes which do not require such skill, ways that athletes themselves can use, or their coach, the basis of which is found in the so-called 'exhaustion methods' for breaking bad habits described previously. Many athletes and coaches have discovered these techniques themselves.

Athletes who, despite repeated instructions to the contrary, persist in performing in ways which interfere with their progress will discover with prolonged practice – that is, with overtraining – that different aspects of their performance from time to time temporarily extinguish. When the faulty ways of performing drop out, and for this reason they briefly realise some of the improvement which they have been seeking, as Knight Dunlap (1932/1972, pp. 204–205) recommends, they should stop. Stopping at this point reinforces the improved behaviour, and tends to preserve it. With rest, of course, the faulty ways of performing will spontaneously recover, and thus the whole process must be repeated at the next training session. As the athletes overtrain again and again, always stopping when the behaviour they are seeking appears, the behaviour they seek will tend to appear earlier and earlier in the training session, and they can then begin to briefly practise the improved behaviour each time it occurs. Athletes must be careful, however, at this stage to limit the extent to which they practise the correct behaviour, in order to avoid the risk of satiating that behaviour. Furthermore, at this stage, though they may have to stay at practice for inconveniently long periods, they must never stop at a time when the improved behaviour is failing to appear. They cannot afford to stop unless they are getting the desired responses. If they stop while not coming up with improved behaviour, the old, faulty behaviour is reinforced, and the athlete's progress may suffer a setback.

Spotting behaviour which is an increment better than previous behaviour and reinforcing it is the mark of a good trainer or coach, and a skill necessary for athletes to have if they expect to somehow train themselves. It is not necessary to know precisely what is wrong with the previous behaviour, how it developed, nor why the athlete persists in continuing it. In using overtraining as a technique for overcoming faulty behaviour, regardless of whether the athletes do so on their own or with the guidance of a coach, it is only necessary to recognise improved behaviour and stop the practice when it occurs. Athletes themselves often have to be the ones who recognise and reinforce their own increments of improvement, but many are those who have become outstanding contenders only because they were fortunate enough to have crucial guidance at times when they had no idea whether or not what they were doing was an improvement over what they had been doing before.

With overtraining, old ways of doing things will from time to time drop out. If as a result of this, new, improved ways of behaving appear *and* are recognised and reinforced, then overtraining can be beneficial. Without this, overtraining poses nothing but hazards to the athlete's future development.

CONCLUSION

Response satiation is a reluctance to continue to repeat the same response. A widely held assumption is that the more work a response takes, the faster satiation builds up. Response satiation, unlike fatigue, is associated only with the response which produced it. The build-up of response satiation accounts for why living organisms must from time to time change what they are doing. Since it is generally assumed that response satiation depends on primitive biological mechanisms common to all animals, it should not be surprising that response satiation, although often under differing names, is repeatedly discovered playing important roles in the behaviour of diverse species over widely diverse situations.

Response satiation seems to be an essential but not sufficient cause of burnout in sport. Burnout in sport is no different from burnout in other categories of human and animal activities, except that burnout in sport is typically easier, because sport, compared to most other activities, takes greater physical energy, more practice of precise movements, and, strange as it may seem, is a great deal more compelling and rewarding. In terms of reversal theory, telic–conformist-dominant athletes are more likely to get extremely involved in their sport, and thus are more likely to practise too much, build up too much response satiation, and burn out. However, most people who discontinue sport do not do so because they burn out. When people drop out of sport, it is usually because they find other things more attractive. But burnout is not the result of finding other activities more attractive; it results because nothing else is attractive at all.

References

Anshel, M. H. (1990) 'Toward validation of a model for coping with acute stress in sport', *International Journal of Sport Psychology* 21: 58–83.

Apter, M. J. (1982) *The Experience of Motivation: The Theory of Psychological Reversals*, London: Academic Press.

Apter, M. J. (1988) 'Beyond the autocentric and the allocentric', in J. H. Kerr, M. J. Apter and M. P. Cowles (eds) *Progress in Reversal Theory*, Amsterdam: Elsevier.

Apter, M. J. (1989) *Reversal Theory: Motivation, Emotion and Personality*, London: Routledge.

Apter, M. J. (1992) *The Dangerous Edge*, New York: Free Press.

Apter, M. J. (1997) 'Reversal theory, stress, and health', in S. Svebak and M. J. Apter (eds) *Stress and Health: A Reversal Theory Perspective*, Washington, DC:Taylor and Francis.

Apter, M. J., Mallows, R. and Williams, S. (1998) 'The development of the Motivational Style Profile', *Personality and Individual Differences* 24: 7–18.

Apter, M. J. and Svebak, S. (1984) 'Type A behaviour and its relationship to seriousmindedness (telic dominance)', *Scandinavian Journal of Psychology* 25: 161–167.

Assagioli, R. (1969, 1990) *Psychosynthesis: A Manual of Principles and Techniques*, London: Mandala.

Au, C., Lindner, K. and Kerr, J. H. (2000) 'Comparison of metamotivational characteristics of basketball and badminton players', paper presented at the Pre-Olympic Congress, Brisbane, September.

Ballard, P. B. (1913) 'Obliviscence and reminiscence', *British Journal of Psychology: Monograph Supplement* 1(2).

Bamber, D., Cockerill, I. M. and Carroll, D. (2000) 'The pathological status of exercise dependence', *British Journal of Sports Medicine* 35: 125–132.

Bar-Eli, M. (1991) 'On the use of paradoxical interventions in counselling and coaching in sport', *The Sport Psychologist* 5: 61–72.

Barr, S. A., McDermott, M. R. and Evans, P. (1990) 'Predicting persistence: a study of telic and paratelic frustration', in J. H. Kerr, S. Murgatroyd and M. J. Apter (eds) *Advances in Reversal Theory*, Amsterdam: Swets and Zeitlinger.

Barron, F. (1969) *Creative Person and Creative Process*, New York: Holt, Rinehart and Winston.

'Battle lines drawn: Aussie bowling to test Indian bats' (1999) *The Japan Times*, 5 May, p. 21.

Best, J. B. (1963) 'Protopsychology', reprinted from *Scientific American*, February, San Francisco: W. H. Freeman.

Bills, A. G. (1931) 'Mental work', *Psychological Bulletin* 28: 505–532.

Blaydon, M. J., Lindner, K. J. and Kerr, J. H. (forthcoming) 'Metamotivational characteristics of eating-disordered and exercise-dependent triathletes', manuscript submitted for publication.

Boutcher, S. H. (1990) 'The role of performance routines in sport', in J. G. Jones and L. Hardy (eds) *Stress and Performance in Sport*, Chichester: Wiley.

Braathen, E. T. and Svebak, S. (1990) 'Task-induced tonic and phasic EMG response patterns and psychological predictors in elite performers of endurance and explosive sports', *International Journal of Psychophysiology* 9: 21–30.

Braathen, E. T. and Svebak, S. (1992) 'Motivational differences among talented teenage athletes: the significance of gender, type of sport and level of excellence', *Scandinavian Journal of Medicine and Science in Sports* 2: 153–159.

Braman, O. R. (1982/1999) *The Oppositional Child*, Indianapolis, IN: Kidsrights.

Braman, O. R. (1988) 'Oppositionalism: clinical descriptions of six forms of telic self-negativism', in M. J. Apter, J. H. Kerr and M. P. Cowles (eds) *Progress in Reversal Theory*, Amsterdam: North-Holland.

Braman, O. R. (1996) 'The role of response satiation in overtraining and burnout in sports', paper presented at the First International Workshop on Motivation and Emotion in Sport: Reversal Theory, Tsukuba, Japan, October.

British Olympic Association (2000) 'The British Olympic Association's position statement on athlete confidentiality', *British Journal of Sports Medicine* 31: 71–72.

Bromley, D. B. (1986) *The Case Study Method in Psychology and Related Disciplines*, London: Wiley.

Brown, R. I. F. (1991) 'Gaming, gambling and other addictive play', in J. H. Kerr and M. J. Apter (eds) *Adult Play: A Reversal Theory Approach*, Amsterdam: Swets and Zeitlinger.

Burton, D. (1988) 'Do anxious swimmers swim slower? Re-examining the elusive anxiety–performance relationship', *Journal of Exercise and Sports Psychology* 10: 45–61.

Burton, D. and Naylor, S. (1997) 'Is anxiety really facilitative? Reaction to the myth that cognitive anxiety always impairs sport performance', *Journal of Applied Sport Psychology* 9: 295–302.

Butler, R. J. and Hardy, L. (1992) 'The performance profile: theory and application', *The Sport Psychologist* 6: 253–264.

Calhoun, J. E. (1995) 'Construct validity of the Telic/Paratelic State Instrument: a measure of reversal theory constructs', unpublished doctoral dissertation, University of Kansas School of Nursing.

Calhoun, J. E. and O'Connell, K. A. (1995) 'Construct validity of the Telic/Paratelic State Instrument: a measure of reversal theory constructs', paper presented at the Seventh International Conference on Reversal Theory, Melbourne, July.

Chapman, C. and DeCastro, J. M. (1990) 'Running addiction: measurement and associated physical characteristics', *Journal of Sports Medicine and Physical Fitness* 30: 283–290.

Chesney, M. A., Eagleston, J. R. and Rosenman, R. H. (1981) 'Type A behaviour: assessment and intervention', in C. K. Prokop and L. A. Bradley (eds) *Medical Psychology: Contributions to Behavioral Medicine*, London: Academic Press.

Chirivella, E. C. and Martinez, L. M. (1994) 'The sensation of risk and motivational tendencies in sports: an empirical study', *Personality and Individual Differences* 16: 777–786.

Clough, P., Hockey, B. and Sewell, D. (1996) 'The use of a diary methodology to assess the impact of exercise on mental states', in C. Robson, B. Cripps and H. Steinberg (eds) *Quality and Quantity: Research Methods in Sport and Exercise Physiology*, Leicester: British Psychological Society.

Coakley, J. (1992) 'Burnout among adolescent athletes: a personal failure or social problem?', *Sociology of Sport Journal* 9: 271–275.

Cogan, N. A. and Brown, R. I. F. (1998) 'Metamotivational dominance, states and injuries in risk and safe sports', *Personality and Individual Differences* 27: 503–518.

Cohen, L. B. (1976) 'Habitualization of infant visual attention', in T. J. Tigue and R. N. Leaton (eds) *Habituation: Perspectives from Child Development, Animal Behavior, and Neurophysiology*, Hillsdale, NJ: Lawrence Erlbaum.

Cook, M. R. and Gerkovich, M. M. (1993) 'The development of a Paratelic Dominance Scale', in J. H. Kerr, S. Murgatroyd and M. J. Apter (eds) *Advances in Reversal Theory*, Amsterdam: Swets and Zeitlinger.

Cook, M. R., Gerkovich, M. M., Potocky, M. and O'Connell, K. (1993) 'Instruments for the assessment of reversal theory states', *Patient Education and Counseling* 22: 99–106.

Cox, T. and Kerr, J. H. (1989) 'Arousal effects during tournament play in squash', *Perceptual and Motor Skills* 69: 1275–1280.

Cox, T. and Kerr, J. H. (1990) 'Self-reported mood in competitive squash', *Personality and Individual Differences* 11(2): 199–203.

Crocker, P. R. E. and Graham, T. R. (1995) 'Coping by competitive athletes with performance stress: gender differences and relationships with affect', *The Sport Psychologist* 9: 325–338.

Curry, T. J. (1992) 'Applying theory Y in sport sociology: redesigning the off-season conditioning program of a big ten swim team', in A. Yiannakis and S. L. Greendorfer (eds) *Applied Sociology of Sport*, Champaign, IL: Human Kinetics.

'Dackell out' (1998) *The Japan Times*, 1 November, p. 22.

'Date tops Pierce to reach Wimbledon semifinals' (1996) *The Japan Times*, 4 June, p. 22.

Davies, S. and West, J. D. (1991) 'A theoretical paradigm for performance enhancement: the multimodal approach', *The Sport Psychologist* 5: 167–174.

'Davis Cup matchups set' (1999) *The Japan Times*, 3 April, p. 22.

de Coverly Veale, D. M. W. (1987) 'Exercise dependence', *British Journal of Addiction* 82: 735–740.

Dempster, F. N. (1988) 'The spacing effect: a case study in the failure to apply the results of psychological results', *American Psychologist* 43: 627–634.

Dennis, W. and Sollenberger, R. T. (1934) 'Negative adaptation in the maze exploration of albino rats', *Journal of Comparative Psychology* 18: 197–206.

Dodge, R. (1923) 'Habituation to rotation', *Journal of Experimental Psychology* 6: 1–35.

Dryden, W. and Feltham, C. (1992) *Brief Counselling: A Practical Guide for Beginning Practitioners*, Buckingham: Open University Press.

Dunlap, K. (1932/1972) *Habits: Their Making and Unmaking*, New York: Liveright.

Ellis, A. (1962) *Reason and Emotion in Psychotherapy*, New York: Lyle Stuart.

Ellis, A. (1970) *The Essence of Rational Psychotherapy: A Comprehensive Approach to Treatment*, New York: Institute for Rational Living.

Eysenck, H. J. (1961) 'Psychosis, drive, and inhibition', *American Journal of Psychiatry* 118: 198–204.

Eysenck, H. J. (1963) 'The measurement of motivation', reprinted from *Scientific American*, May, San Francisco: W. H. Freeman.

Fontana, D. (1991) 'Reversals and the Eastern religious mind', in J. H. Kerr and M. J. Apter (eds) *Adult Play: A Reversal Theory Approach*, Amsterdam: Swets and Zeitlinger.

Fontana, D. and Valente, L. (1993) 'Reversal theory, drama and psychological health', in J. H. Kerr, S. Murgatroyd and M. J. Apter (eds) *Advances in Reversal Theory*, Lisse: Swets and Zeitlinger.

Fontana, D. and Valente, L. (1997a) 'Stress in the workplace: causes and treatments', in S. Svebak and M. J. Apter (eds) *Stress and Health: A Reversal Theory Perspective*, Washington, DC: Taylor and Francis.

Fontana, D. and Valente, L. (1997b) 'Drama therapy and the theory of psychological reversals', *The Arts in Psychotherapy* 20: 133–142.

Ford, D. (1998) 'Focus on the ball', *Rugby World*, March, p. 90.

Foxman, J. (1972) 'Effect of cognitive rehearsal on rat phobic behavior', *Journal of Abnormal Psychology* 79: 39–46.

Francis, R. D. (1999) *Ethics for Psychologists: A Handbook*, Leicester: British Psychological Society Books.

Frankl, V. E. (1960) 'Paradoxical intention: a logotherapeutic technique', *American Journal of Psychotherapy* 14: 520–535.

Frankl, V. (1973) *Psychotherapy and Existentialism: Selected Papers on Logotherapy*, Harmondsworth: Penguin.

Garner, D. M. and Garfinkel, P. E. (1979) 'The Eating Attitudes Test: an index of the symptoms of anorexia nervosa', *Psychological Medicine* 9: 273–279.

'Gebreselassie, Szabo break 5,000M marks' (1998) *The Japan Times*, 16 February, p. 24.

Gill, D. L. and Deeter, T. E. (1988) 'Development of the Sport Orientation Questionnaire', *Research Quarterly for Exercise and Sport* 59: 191–202.

Glickman, J. (1998) 'Joy and pain: the Zen of the "erg"', *The Tribune*, 20 January, p. 17.

Gould, D., Eklund, R. C. and Jackson, S. A. (1993) 'Coping strategies used by more and less successful US Olympic wrestlers', *Research Quarterly for Exercise and Sport* 64: 83–93.

Gould, D., Udry, E., Tuffney, S. and Loehr, J. (1996a) 'Burnout in competitive junior tennis players: I. A quantitative psychological assessment', *The Sport Psychologist* 10: 322–340.

Gould, D., Tuffney, S., Udry, E. and Loehr, J. (1996b) 'Burnout in competitive junior tennis players: II. A qualitative analysis', *The Sport Psychologist* 10: 341–366.

Gould, D., Tuffney, S., Udry, E. and Loehr, J. (1997) 'Burnout in competitive junior tennis players: III. Individual differences in the burnout experience', *The Sport Psychologist* 11: 257–276.

Guthrie, E. R. (1935) *The Psychology of Learning*, New York: Harper.

Heil, J. (1993) 'A psychologist's view of the personal challenge of injury', in J. Heil (ed.) *Psychology of Sport Injury*, Champaign, IL: Human Kinetics.

'Hen-mania hits Wimbledon: British crowd boisterous in backing of local boy' (1997) *The Japan Times*, 1 July, p. 24.

Hollander, D. B., Meyers, M. C. and LeUnes, A. (1995) 'Psychological factors associated with overtraining: implications for youth sport coaches', *Journal of Sport Behavior* 1: 3–20.

Hull, C. L. (1943) *Principles of Behavior*, New York: Appleton-Century-Crofts.

'Injured skier says crash leaves her full of fear' (1996) *The Japan Times*, 18 February, p. 22.

'I owe you a debt that only victory can repay' (1997) *The Express*, 4 July, p. 3.

Jacobson, P. (1974) *Progressive Relaxation*, Chicago: University of Chicago Press.

Jones, G. and Swain, A. B. J. (1992) 'Intensity and direction dimensions of competitive state anxiety and relationships with competitiveness', *Perceptual and Motor Skills* 74: 467–472.

Jones, G. and Swain, A. B. J. (1995) 'Predispositions to experience debilitative and facilitative anxiety in elite and non-elite performers', *The Sport Psychologist* 9(2): 201–211.

Kerr, J. H. (1987) 'Differences in the motivational characteristics of "professional", "serious amateur" and "recreational" sports performers', *Perceptual and Motor Skills* 64: 379–382.

Kerr, J. H. (1988) 'A study of motivation in rugby', *Journal of Social Psychology* 128(2): 269–270.

Kerr, J. H. (1991) 'Arousal-seeking in risk sport participants', *Personality and Individual Differences* 12(6): 613–616.

Kerr, J. H. (1993) 'An eclectic approach to psychological interventions in sport: reversal theory', *The Sport Psychologist* 7: 400–418.

Kerr, J. H. (1994) *Understanding Soccer Hooliganism*, Buckingham: Open University Press.

Kerr, J. H. (1997) *Motivation and Emotion in Sport: Reversal Theory*, Hove: Psychology Press.

Kerr, J. H. (ed.) (1999) *Experiencing Sport: Reversal Theory*, Chichester: Wiley.

Kerr, J. H. and Apter, M. J. (1999) 'The State of Mind Indicator for Athletes', in J. H. Kerr (ed.) *Experiencing Sport: Reversal Theory*, Chichester: Wiley.

Kerr, J. H. and Cox, T. (1988) 'Effects of telic dominance and metamotivational state on squash task performance', *Perceptual and Motor Skills* 67: 171–174.

Kerr, J. H. and Cox, T. (1990) 'Cognition and mood in relation to the performance of a squash task', *Acta Psychologica* 73(1): 103–114.

Kerr, J. H. and Svebak, S. (1989) 'Motivational aspects of preference for, and participation in, "risk" and "safe" sports', *Personality and Individual Differences* 10: 797–800.

Kerr, J. H. and Svebak, S. (1994) 'The acute effects of participation in sports on mood', *Personality and Individual Differences* 16(1): 159–166.

Kerr, J. H. and Tacon, P. (1999) 'Psychological responses to different types of locations and activities', *Journal of Environmental Psychology* 19: 287–294.

Kerr, J. H. and van den Wollenberg, A. E. (1997) 'High and low intensity exercise and psychological mood states', *Psychology and Health* 12(5): 603–618.

Kerr, J. H. and van Lienden, H. J. (1987) 'Telic dominance in masters swimmers', *Scandinavian Journal of Sports Sciences* 9(3): 85–88.

Kerr, J. H. and van Schaik, P. (1995) 'Effects of game venue and outcome on psychological mood states in rugby', *Personality and Individual Differences* 19(3): 407–410

Kerr, J. H. and Vlaswinkel, E. H. (1993) 'Self-reported mood and running under natural conditions', *Work and Stress* 7(2): 161–177.

Kientzle, M. J. (1946) 'Properties of learning curves under varied distributions of practice', *Journal of Experimental Psychology* 36: 187–211.

Klein, D. (1990) 'Anxiety and sport performance: a meta-analysis', *Anxiety Research* 2: 113–131.

Krane, V. and Williams, J. (1987) 'Performance and somatic anxiety, cognitive anxiety, and confidence changes prior to competition', *Journal of Sport Behavior* 10(1): 47–56.

Kremer, J. and Scully, D. (1994) *Psychology in Sport*, London: Taylor and Francis.

Lafreniere, K., Cowles, M. P. and Apter, M. J. (1988) 'The reversal phenomenon: reflections on a laboratory study', in M. J. Apter, J. H. Kerr and M. P. Cowles (eds) *Progress in Reversal Theory*, Advances in Psychology Series 51, Amsterdam: North-Holland/Elsevier.

Lafreniere, K. D., Ledgerwood, D. M. and Murgatroyd, S. (2001) 'Psychopathology, therapy and counselling', in M. J. Apter (ed.) *Motivational Styles in Everyday Life: A Guide to Reversal Theory*, Washington, DC: American Psychological Association.

Lazarus, A. A. (1981) *The Practice of Multi-modal Therapy*, New York: McGraw-Hill.

Lepley, W. M. and Rice, G. M., Jr (1952) 'Behavior variability in paramecia as a function of act sequences', *Journal of Comparative Physiology and Psychology* 5: 283–286.

McCann, S. (1995) 'Overtraining and burnout', in S. M. Murphy (ed.) *Sport Psychology Interventions*, Champaign, IL: Human Kinetics.

McDermott, M. R. and Apter, M. J. (1988) 'The Negativism Dominance Scale', in M. J. Apter, J. H. Kerr and M. P. Cowles (eds) *Progress in Reversal Theory*, Advances in Psychology Series 51, Amsterdam: North-Holland/Elsevier.

Madden, C. C., Summers, J. J. and Brown, D. F. (1990) 'The influence of perceived stress on coping with competitive basketball', *International Journal of Sport Psychology* 21: 21–35.

Males, J. R. (1995) 'Helping athletes perform: integrating reversal theory and psychosynthesis in applied sport psychology', paper presented at the Seventh International Conference on Reversal Theory, Melbourne, July.

Males, J. R. (1996) 'A comparison of pre-competitive mood and stress in elite male lacrosse and volleyball players', paper presented at the First International Workshop on Motivation and Emotion in Sport: Reversal Theory, Tsukuba, Japan, October.

Males, J. R. (1999) 'Individual experience in slalom canoeing', in J. H. Kerr (ed.) *Experiencing Sport: Reversal Theory*, Chichester: Wiley.

Males, J. R. and Kerr, J. H. (1996) 'Stress, emotion and performance in elite slalom canoeists', *The Sport Psychologist* 10: 17–36.

Males, J. R., Kerr, J. H. and Gerkovich, M. (1998) 'Metamotivational states during canoe slalom competition: a qualitative analysis using reversal theory', *Journal of Applied Sport Psychology* 10: 184–200.

Man, F., Stuchlíková, I. and Kindlmann, P. (1995) 'Trait–state anxiety, worry, emotionality and self-confidence in top-level soccer players', *The Sport Psychologist* 9(2): 212–224.

Martens, R. (1977) *Sport Competition Anxiety Test*, Champaign, IL: Human Kinetics.

Martin, R. A., Kuiper, N. A., Olinger, L. J. and Dobbin, J. (1987) 'Is stress always bad? Telic versus paratelic dominance as a stress moderating variable', *Journal of Personality and Social Psychology* 53: 970–982.

Miller, W. R. (1985) 'Addictive behavior and the theory of psychological. reversals', *Addictive Behaviors* 10: 177–180.

'More at stake than cricket supremacy in World Cup final' (1999) *The Japan Times*, 20 June, p. 22.

Morris, T. and Summers, J. (1995) *Sport Psychology: Theory, Applications and Issues*, Chichester: Wiley.

Murgatroyd, S. J. (1981) 'Reversal theory: a new perspective on crisis counselling', *British Journal of Guidance and Counselling* 9: 180–193.

Murgatroyd, S. J. (1987a) 'Humour as a tool in counselling and psychotherapy: a reversal-theory perspective', *British Journal of Guidance and Counselling* 15: 225–236.

Murgatroyd, S. J. (1987b) 'Depression and structural-phenomenological eclectic psychotherapy: the case of Gill', in J. Norcross (ed.) *Casebook of Brief Psychotherapy*, New York: Brunner/Mazel.

Murgatroyd, S. J. (1987c) 'Reversal theory and psychotherapy: a review', *Counselling Psychology Quarterly* 1: 57–74.

Murgatroyd, S. and Apter, M. J. (1984) 'Eclectic psychotherapy: a structural–phenomenological approach', in W. Dryden (ed.) *Individual Psychotherapy in Britain*, London: Harper and Row.

Murgatroyd, S. and Apter, M. J. (1986) 'A structural-phenomenological approach to eclectic psychotherapy', in J. Norcross (ed.) *Handbook of Eclectic Psychotherapy*, New York: Brunner/Mazel.

Murgatroyd, S., Rushton, C., Apter, M. J. and Ray, C. (1978) 'The development of the Telic Dominance Scale', *Journal of Personality Assessment* 42: 519–528.

Murphy, S. M. (eds) (1995) *Sport Psychology Interventions*, Champaign, IL: Human Kinetics.

O'Connell, K. A., Gerkovich, M. M. and Cook, M. R. (1997) 'Relapse crises during smoking cessation', in S. Svebak and M. J. Apter (eds) *Stress and Health: A Reversal Theory Perspective*, Washington, DC: Taylor and Francis.

Ogden, J., Veale, D. M. W. and Summers, Z. (1997) 'The development and validation of the Exercise Dependence Questionnaire', *Addiction Research* 5: 343–356.

Ohmura, Y. (1999) 'Greene leaves Ito standing still in 100', *The Japan Times*, 16 September, p. 22.

'Olympic veteran to lead Canada's team at Games' Atlanta opening' (1996) *The Vancouver Sun*, 7 July, p. 1.

Pavlov, I. P. (1926/1960) *Conditioned Reflexes*, trans. G. V. Anrep, New York: Dover.

Pepitas, A. J., Giges, B. and Danish, S. J. (1999) 'The sport psychologist–athlete relationship: implications for training', *The Sport Psychologist* 13: 344–357.

Perkins, D., Wilson, G. and Kerr, J. H. (2001) 'The effects of elevated arousal and mood on maximal strength performance in athletes', *Journal of Applied Sport Psychology*, in press.

Perna, F., Neyer, M., Murphy, S. M., Ogilvie, B. C. and Murphy, A. (1995) 'Consultations with sport organizations: a cognitive–behavioural model', in S. M. Murphy (ed.) *Sport Psychology Interventions*, Champaign, IL: Human Kinetics.

Peters, M. and Woolridge, I. (1974) *Mary P.: Autobiography*, London: Paul.

Petlichkoff, L. M. (1996) 'The drop-out dilemma in youth sports', in O. Bar Or (ed.) *The Encyclopedia of Sport Medicine*, vol. 6: *The Child and Adolescent Athlete*, Oxford: Blackwell.

Pierce, E. F. (1994) 'Exercise dependence syndrome in runners', *Sports Medicine* 18: 149–155.

'Player suspends himself for racism' (1999) *The Japan Times*, 11 April, p. 21.

Purcell, I. P. (1999) 'Verbal protocols and structured interviews for motives, plans and decisions in golf', in J. H. Kerr (ed.) *Experiencing Sport: Reversal Theory*, Chichester: Wiley.

Raglin, J. S. and Turner, P. E. (1993) 'Anxiety and performance in track and field athletes: a comparison of the inverted-U hypothesis with zone of optimal function theory', *Personality and Individual Differences* 14: 163–171.

Richman, C. L. (1989) 'SAB, reward, and learning', in W. N. Dember and C. L. Richman (eds) *Spontaneous Alternation Behavior*, New York: Springer-Verlag.

Ryan, J. (1996) *Little Girls in Pretty Boxes: The Making and Breaking of Elite Gymnasts and Figure Skaters*, London: The Women's Press.

Sechenov, I. M. (1863/1965) *Reflexes of the Brain*, trans. L. Belsky, Cambridge, MA: MIT Press.

Smaal, R. (1998) 'Hasek reigns supreme as Czechs clinch gold: Russians unable to beat star goalie', *The Japan Times*, 23 February, p. 24.

Smith, R. E. (1986) 'Toward a cognitive–affective model of athletic burnout', *Journal of Sport Psychology* 8: 36–50.

Spielberger, C. D., Gorsuch, R. L. and Lushene, R. E. (1970) *Manual for the State–Trait Anxiety Inventory*, Palo Alto, CA: Consulting Psychologists Press.

Stafford, I. (1999) 'Trading places', *Rugby World*, February, pp. 42–49.

'Stars claim Cup in OT thriller' (1999) *The Japan Times*, 21 June, p. 24.

Stumpfl, T. G. and Levis, D. J. (1967) 'Essentials of implosive therapy: a learning-theory-based psychodynamic behavioral therapy', *Journal of Abnormal Psychology* 72: 496–503.

Summers, J. and Stewart, E. (1993) 'The arousal performance relationship: examining different conceptions', in S. Serpa, J. Alves, V. Ferriera and A. Paula-Brito (eds) *Proceedings of the Eighth World Congress of Sport Psychology*, Lisbon: International Society of Sport Psychology.

Svebak, S. (1984) 'Active and passive forearm flexor tension patterns in the continuous perceptual–motor task paradigm: the significance of motivation', *International Journal of Psychophysiology* 2, 167–176.

Svebak, S. (1993) 'The development of the Tension and Effort Stress Inventory (TESI)', in J. H. Kerr, S. Murgatroyd and M. J. Apter (eds) *Advances in Reversal Theory*, Amsterdam: Swets and Zeitlinger.

Svebak, S. (1997) 'Tension- and effort-stress as predictors of academic performance', in S. Svebak and M. J. Apter (eds) *Stress and Health: A Reversal Theory Perspective*, Washington, DC: Taylor and Francis.

Svebak, S. and Apter, M. J. (1997) *Stress and Health: A Reversal Theory Perspective*, Washington, DC: Taylor and Francis.

Svebak, S. and Kerr, J. H. (1989) 'The role of impulsivity in preference for sports', *Personality and Individual Differences* 10(1): 51–58.

Svebak, S. and Murgatroyd, S. (1985) 'Metamotivational dominance: a multi-method validation of reversal theory constructs', *Journal of Personality and Social Psychology* 48(1): 107–116.

Svebak, S., Storfjell, O. and Dalen, K. (1982) 'The effect of a threatening context upon motivation and task-induced physiological changes', *British Journal of Psychology* 73: 505–512.

Svebak, S., Ursin, H., Endresen, I., Hjelmen, A. M. and Apter, M. J. (1991) 'Psychological factors in the aetiology of back pain', *Psychology and Health* 5: 307–314.

Swain, A. B. J. and Jones, G. (1993) 'Intensity and frequency dimensions of competitive state anxiety', *Journal of Sports Sciences* 11: 533–542.

Swoap, R. A. and Murphy, S. M. (1995) 'Eating disorders and weight management in athletes', in S. M. Murphy (ed.) *Sport Psychology Interventions*, Champaign, IL: Human Kinetics.

Syer, J. and Connolly, C. (1984) *Sporting Mind Sporting Body: An Athlete's Guide to Mental Training*, New York: Cambridge University Press.

Terry, P. C. (1995) 'The efficacy of mood state profiling among elite performers', *The Sport Psychologist* 9: 309–324.

Thayer, R. E. (1989) *The Biopsychology of Mood and Arousal*, New York: Oxford University Press.

Thorndike, E. L. (1914/1949) 'Mental fatigue', in E. L. Thorndike, *Selected Writings from a Connectionist's Psychology*, New York: Greenwood Press.

'Thys runs second-best marathon' (1998) *The Japan Times*, 16 February, p. 24.

Torild Hellandsig, E. (1998) 'Motivational predictors of high performance and discontinuation in different types of sports among talented teenage athletes', *International Journal of Sport Psychology* 29: 27–44.

'Tyson admits he crossed the line, tasted blood' (1998) *The Japan Times*, 13 January, p. 20.

Van Raalte, J. L., Brewer, B. W., Rivera, P. M. and Pepitas, A. J. (1994) 'The relationship between observable self-talk and competitive junior tennis players' match performances', *Journal of Sport and Exercise Psychology* 16: 400–415.

Varcoe, F. (1999) 'Sugiyama advances to quarters: Krajicek, Enqvist also straight-set winners at Japan Open', *The Japan Times*, 16 April, p. 24.

Veale, D. M. W. (1995) 'Does primary exercise dependence really exist?', in J. Annett, B. Cripps and H. Steinberg (eds) *Exercise Addiction: Motivation for Participation in Sport and Exercise. Proceedings of a British Psychological Society, Sport and Exercise Psychology Section Workshop*, Leicester: British Psychological Society.

'Villeneuve says racing "too safe"' (1997) *The Japan Times*, 2 February, p. 21.

Vlaswinkel, E. H. and Kerr, J. H. (1990) 'Negativism dominance in risk and team sports', *Perceptual and Motor Skills* 70: 288–290.

Ward, L. B. (1937) 'Reminiscence and rote learning', *Psychological Monograph* 49(220).

Weber, B. (1998) 'Forever Young', *Coach and Athletic Director*, October, pp. 41–49.

Welland, C. (1996) 'Pure pleasure the cure for poison of jingoism', *Guardian, Sports Week Supplement*, 17 March, p. 2.

Williams, D. (1995) 'Freddie Fittler's day off', *Inside Sport*, June, pp. 90–101.

Wilson, G. V. (1999) 'Success, failure and emotional experience in sport', in J. H. Kerr (ed.) *Experiencing Sport: Reversal Theory*, Chichester: Wiley.

Wilson, G. V. and Kerr, J. H. (1999) 'Affective responses to success and failure: a study of winning and losing in competitive rugby', *Personality and Individual Differences* 27: 85–99.

Wilson, G. V. and Phillips, M. (1995) 'A reversal theory explanation of emotions in competitive sport', paper presented at the Seventh International Conference on Reversal Theory, Melbourne, July.

Wolpe, J. (1958) *Psychotherapy by Reciprocal Inhibition*, Stanford, CA: Stanford University Press.

Woodworth, R. S. (1921) *Psychology: A Study of Mental Life*, New York: Holt.

Young, P. T. (1936) *Motivation of Behavior*, New York: Wiley.

Zeaman, D. and House, B. J. (1951) 'The growth and decay of reactive inhibition as measured by alternation behavior', *Journal of Experimental Psychology* 41: 177–186.

Author Index

Subject Index